Teaching Research in Design

Design, Vol. 58

Acknowledgement:
Our thanks go to the sociologists Julia Pintsuk-Christof, M.A., who supported us significantly during the implementation of the research project RIDE and Dr. Anna Wanka, who advised us with her expertise during the application and conception process of the project.
Furthermore, we would like to thank Kristin Weißenberger and the team of "handgedacht" as well as all students of the study program "Manual & Material Culture" for their willingness to actively participate in the experiments and to be available for the surveys and interviews.

Bibliographic information published by the Deutsche Nationalbibliothek

The Deutsche Nationalbibliothek lists this publication in the Deutsche Nationalbibliografie; detailed bibliographic data are available in the Internet at http://dnb.d-nb.de

© 2023 transcript Verlag, Bielefeld

Cover layout & cover illustration: Andreas Pawlik, Bernhard Poppe and Manuel Radde
            for dform.at, Vienna
Book design: Manuel Radde for dform.at, Vienna
Typeset: Simon Hundsbichler for dform.at, Vienna
Typefaces: ES Face (extraset.ch), Lektorat (Florian Fecher for typetogether, 2020),
            Triangular (Bernhard Poppe for dform.at, 2022)
Proofread: Übersetzungsbüro Andrea Kraus, Graz

Printed by Majuskel Medienproduktion GmbH, Wetzlar
Print-ISBN 978-3-8376-6376-1
PDF-ISBN 978-3-8394-6376-5
https://doi.org/10.14361/9783839463765
ISSN of series: 2702-8801
eISSN of series: 2702-881X

Sandra Dittenberger   Hans Stefan Moritsch   Agnes Raschauer

Teaching

Research

in Design

Guidelines for Integrating Scientific
Standards in Design Education

[transcript] Design

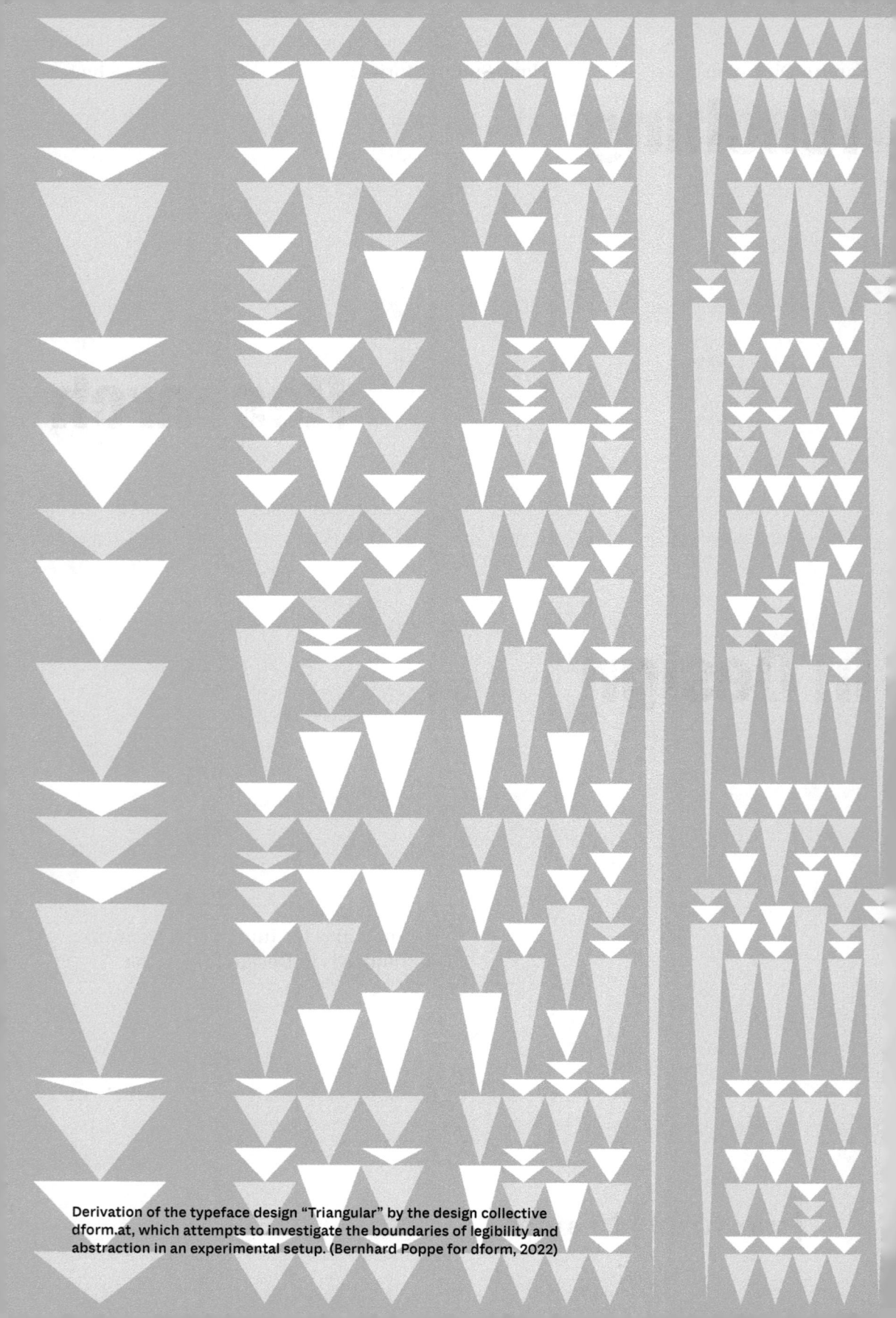

Derivation of the typeface design "Triangular" by the design collective
dform.at, which attempts to investigate the boundaries of legibility and
abstraction in an experimental setup. (Bernhard Poppe for dform, 2022)

Theory Overview

Research Project

A   Introduction

The term research in connection with design is now well established among both theorists and practitioners in their daily working lives. Yes, the term indeed seems to be almost ubiquitous, but it also evokes a wide range of thoughts and associations among representatives of both fields. Upon closer examination, it becomes clear that a variety of definitions exist for both research and design. Thus, even in design education, teachers and students alike have different views on what research in design means and how it should be conducted. From the point of view of design teachers, addressing research in design has become an important aspect of every curriculum. When is it best to introduce this area to students? To what extent should research be taught in the long-established system of practice-based design studio teaching? What definition of research should be followed and what research methodology is most appropriate? How can students be motivated to consider research as part of their daily design work? This series of questions formed the starting point for a three-year research project titled "Research in Design Education: Artistic-Scientific Research in Design Teaching Practice", which was conducted by design and design research educators as well as social scientists at the New Design University in St. Pölten, Lower Austria in the "Manual & Material Culture" BA programme between 2019-2022.

Design research and design practice have become intertwined in a new way over the previous decades. Since the 1990s, academic debate has revolved around the question of how to define research agendas in design. As a result, different strands of the debates have arrived at differing notions of what design research is, how it may best be put into practice, and which methods are to be used. The integration of research in design practice is therefore not a new topic in itself in the academic context today. However, the implementation of these approaches in everyday design practice remains a major challenge.

Across the university landscape of design education around the globe, it can be observed that different approaches have been found for integrating research into design work. At the same time, the different interpretations of how research is practiced in the field of design prove to be a problem. This becomes especially evident within the realm of practice-based design research, leading to severe disagreements. Jorge Frascara pointed out, already in 2007, that "the use of the word 'research' to refer to activities devoid of method [...] could be called 'explorations'. Without method, there is no research" (ibid., p. 65). To this date, the integration of research into design practice has not been conceptualised in a satisfactory manner within academic design discourse. Its implementation in design study programmes can be severely criticised:

> "[...] universities require staff to develop research activity, it has become common to add the term 'research' to the practice of design. Design instructors, hiding behind myths that exist in popular culture about art, describe their run-of-the-mill design practice as 'design research.' The ordinary practice of design, however, is not necessarily research" (ibid., p. 62).

Although many years have passed since this statement was made, the field of practice-based design research is still faced with the challenge of answering the question of how new knowledge is created through practical designing and which scientific standards have to be met when carrying out design research.

In addition to this still unresolved question, how designers themselves understand research is also an important aspect. Over the last three decades, design research has been a topic of discussion within design practice, yet these two thematic landscapes have been practised more alongside each other than interwoven, resulting in genuine difficulties concerning the building of bridges between theory and practice in design. Hockey (2008) described that students with a design practice background found the experience of entering the academic world, and the necessity of being able to write academic texts and provide theoretical contextualisation, to be a reality shock and threat to their artistic identity. This finding can be confirmed by teaching experience from the BA level on, where students experience research-related tasks as conflicting with their identities as creative individuals. Scientific-methodological work is perceived as impacting negatively on the creative process. However, the ability to reflect on one's own creative work seems to be a crucial skill for design students to productively combine analytical-methodological with creative-artistic practices in their design process. To prepare students for further study programmes like master's or PhD programmes as well as contemporary inter- and transdisciplinary design practice, it is essential to establish an awareness and understanding of the need to establish an active knowledge bridge between research and design practice during their BA studies. Design education has to develop solutions for this new demand and support these profound changes in the discipline itself by addressing these issues from the very beginning of design education, i.e., at the BA level.

A number of developments have contributed to the growing interest in developing learning formats in which design students engage with research. Among them, the diversification of contexts in which designers work, for example, as consultants, with policy makers, in close collaboration with other fields, as well as the impact digital technologies have on design practice. According to Vaughan (2019b), these changes have a huge effect on how design itself is understood and conducted, and they also create a new role for design research (ibid., p. 1). "All these innovations in contexts, methods and applications of design are calling for a new kind of designer, or at least an expanded capacity to undertake research with increasing sophistication" (ibid.). Design study programmes have to react to these changes, equipping students with the ability to link their creative practice with design research. Which, as a result, also creates a "need for design educators to transform their own design practices and pedagogic capacities" (ibid.) to meet this challenge.

The list of hurdles to overcome when trying to merge the fields of research and design practice is long. As briefly mentioned above, there is a broad landscape of definitions related to design and research in design. Which profession do we focus on in this book, and to whom is it addressed?

When we speak of design in this publication, we are addressing the profession of product design, and we are addressing design as well as design research educators. We are well aware that there are already many publications available that try to introduce designers to traditional research methodologies and methods. This publication is not intended to contribute to "scientifying" the intuitive and implicit processes of design. Rather, it aims to define the scientific aspects of design research and to offer specific guidance for design teaching that will make it easier for students and teachers to integrate scientific ways of working into design practice in a productive way that is accessible to other disciplines. A basic understanding of the differences between design, research, and science and their significance in different phases of a holistic design process is the basis for being able to position oneself as a design expert confidently and competently in both research and practice. For this reason, this publication attempts to build a living bridge between design practice and design research and to generate a holistic design process consisting of both aspects. This does not in any way question the necessity of teaching in the practised design studio culture and theory courses, but rather attempts to experience product design as a design, research, and experimental process in order to prepare students for mastering future design tasks in an increasingly complex world.

Consequently, this publication is set within the realm of design education research and focuses on the question of how to integrate design research into design education at the undergraduate level, arguing for the necessity to specify standards which are to be met in order for practice-based design research to be classified as such.

The motivation for this book was to document the knowledge journey we undertook during the research project and, we hope, to make a useful contribution to the efforts to bring students into contact with research from the beginning of their academic design education and to present possibilities for implementing research into design study programmes.

The research project set itself the goal of finding out how design and science can be shaped and interwoven in order to build the necessary knowledge bridge between theory, empiricism, and design practice within the framework of research-led teaching in bachelor's degree programmes. The main focus was to find out how research work can be defined at the BA level and which competences students would need to conduct design research. Furthermore, questions like which research approach should be chosen for research-based project work in order to support the design process, which teaching concepts or didactic formats support the process of research-based project work and, finally, whether a holistic presentation of theory, empiricism, and design practice, in the sense of a design process guide, already exists were posed.

This publication traces the milestones of the research project and presents the results in three parts: part I – theory overview, part II – the research project, and part III – a guideline for teaching research in design.

Part I, theory overview, delineates different positions on research in design. Chapter B starts with an overview of the definition of scientific research according to the *Frascati Manual* (OECD, 2015), the topic of research-based learning, and a discussion of the different types of design research. Furthermore, this chapter shows what research currently being conducted in product design can be found in the literature and specifically addresses the areas of practice-based and practice-led research. It also presents information gathered on the scientific standards to be followed in design research. It concludes with a consideration of how the research schemes of scientific research and design research can be related. As already mentioned, students may experience the involvement of research in their practice-based project work as a restriction of their creative freedom. The literature review in chapter C on the discussion about the process and required content of practice-based research projects at the PhD level shows that there is obviously little design pedagogical engagement with the integration of research at the BA level.

<u>Part II, research project</u>, shows that students in the final year of the "Manual & Material Culture" BA programme experience substantial difficulties integrating design research into their final projects. These difficulties in combining scientific-methodological approaches with creative tasks result from having to translate a general notion of design research to specific design projects. Assessing students' main competencies and competence development over the course of their studies, it is suggested that students need ample time and experience for the connection between research and practice to become self-evident. The application of structured design processes and their reflection must be taught and practiced from the beginning of the students' studies on. Experiments aimed at investigating ways of generating knowledge through practical design action indicate that scientific design research is not easily found in practical action / the 'daily business' of product designers, as all the necessary conditions to meet scientific research standards are lacking.

<u>Part III, teaching research in design</u>, introduces a way of recombining existing processes and methods in order to suggest two approaches for conducting research in product design practice. ◄

Theory Overview

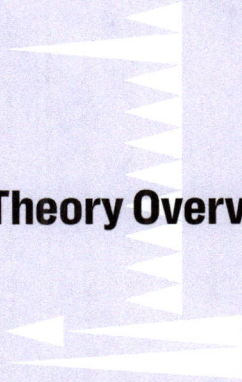

B   Comparing positions:
   What is considered as research in design?

In the discourse on research in design, design positions itself at the interface between art and science. Designers design, research, and develop project-related strategies in order to deal with complex issues, taking into account a wide range of interests. Design has established itself as an independent and flexible discipline. The areas in which designers contribute their skills or in which design practices are used are becoming increasingly diverse. Designers are neither artists nor scientists. Rather, they integrate artistic and scientific methods into their working process and enter into project-related collaborations with experts from a wide range of fields. The increasing complexity of many tasks makes it necessary to carry out research during the planning phase of a project on which methodology makes sense for the respective task. The basic prerequisite for sustainable design work is openness to new tasks and the willingness to make disciplines that lack their own expertise accessible through cooperation with experts, thereby constantly developing its own method catalogue. The legitimate claim that design practice is recognised as research must also go hand in hand with the willingness not to hide behind the axiom of a indescribable artistic knowledge (Badura et al., 2015).

   Within the field of design, the potential to extract new knowledge through practice has already given rise to many attempts at a definition. In 1993, Frayling described this endeavour as "research-through-design"; in 2002, Biggs described it as "practice-based research"; in 2009, Bonsiepe coined the term "endogenous design research" for it; in 2011, Koskinen, Zimmerman, Binder, Redström, and Wensveen returned to the constructive roots of design and gave it the term "constructive design research"; and in 2013, Dorst called it "academic design". Krogh and Koskinen (2020) have identified four epistemic traditions in constructive design research: experiential, methodical, programmatic, and dialectic. The experiential tradition understands artefacts as knowledge, meaning that objects result from a design process. The methodical tradition understands discourse as knowledge, in which programmes and theoretical frameworks act as foundations of design decisions. The programmatic tradition understands participation as knowledge, where scientific measures are applied to help assess the quality and validity of the design intention. Finally, the dialectic tradition understands the mutual learning between experts and amateurs as knowledge.

Within the field of design education, universities strive to enhance the connection between research and teaching and forms of learning by research have become popular among university teachers. Learning by research denotes a broad field of related but distinct formats for structuring students' learning processes. In a basic sense, they all imply that students engage in an active way with some elements of a research process, for example, working on a research question they themselves posed, using scientific methods and concepts, and assessing their course of action in a critical manner (Huber, 2013). A concept that is widely used in the creative arts and that may be linked to learning by research is practice-based research. This approach, too, is not defined in a uniform way, since various definitions are used in different disciplines. For Candy and Edmonds (2018), the key defining element of practice-based research is that results may easily be incorporated into existing and emerging practice. The results of practice-based research must further transcend the specific context in which they emerged for the research to be relevant as such.

In order to get started with the investigation of the question, the definitions of scientific research and learning by research were first examined, as they have a long tradition in scientific practice. Furthermore, it became clear through the examination of the main topic of the chapter that many different terms are used in the literature to describe research activities in design, such as "artistic-scientific research", "design research", "practice-based research", and "practice-led research". In the sense of a comparison of positions, the individual terms are presented in the following subchapters and examined for their similarities and differences.

B1   Forms of scientific research

Within the *Frascati Manual* of the OECD (2015), research and experimental development (R&D) is defined as "creative and systematic work undertaken in order to increase the stock of knowledge – including knowledge of humankind, culture and society – and to devise new applications of available knowledge" (ibid., p. 44). Research activities should meet the five core criteria of being "novel, creative, uncertain, systematic, transferable and/or reproducible" (ibid., p. 45).

In addition to the definition of R&D and its core criteria, the *Frascati Manual* divides research activities into three areas:
- Basic research is experimental or theoretical work undertaken primarily to acquire new knowledge of the underlying foundations of phenomena and observable facts, without any particular application or use in view.
- Applied research is original investigation undertaken in order to acquire new knowledge. It is, however, directed primarily towards a specific, practical aim or objective.

► "Experimental development is systematic work, drawing on knowledge gained from research and practical experience and producing additional knowledge, which is directed to producing new products or processes or to improving existing products or processes" ([emphasis in original] ibid., p. 45)."

Concerning the differentiation of R&D, information is offered for disciplines like the natural sciences and engineering and the social sciences, humanities, and the arts. Within the latter, there is an indication of a possible "blurring of boundaries [which] could affect the distinction between basic and applied research" (ibid., p. 55). Furthermore, it is noted that difficulties of classification could also arise in the area of experimental development due to the nature of the disciplines involved.

R&D activities related to design are also described as difficult to separate with regard to the core criteria of novelty and uncertainty. Nevertheless, it is emphasised that "[d]esign plays a key role in the development and implementation of innovations" (ibid., p. 63). Design is acknowledged to contribute to innovations when planning new products or processes. This therefore meets the criterion of novelty to a certain extent. However, the fulfilment of the criterion of uncertainty is strongly questioned. The planning of a building is used here as an example. From the start of the project, there is no question that in the end a building will actually be designed. Thus, there is no uncertainty about the outcome of the research (ibid., p. 64). It is stated that "design is not R&D and [...] has to be kept distinct from R&D for any statistical purpose" (ibid.). Based on the example of the design of a building, the additional tasks within such a project, like the time and cost factor, may fulfil the criterion of uncertainty (ibid.).

Since design is often described through the use of artistic methods which could represent a bridge to research, these areas are briefly outlined. "Research for the arts" (ibid., p. 65) is mentioned as the first area and is described through the development of new goods or services that are needed for the implementation of artistic work. Based on basic and/or applied research, the second area is titled "[r]esearch on the arts" (ibid., p. 65) and includes the field of studies on artistic expression. In contrast, the areas of "[a]rtistic expression" (ibid., p. 65) and artistic performance as such are excluded from the field of R&D because they do not meet the criteria of novelty and reproducibility. Furthermore, it is stated that higher education institutions, which offer PhD programmes, should develop an appropriate research approach that can be identified and recognised as R&D. "[A]rts colleges and university arts departments cannot be assumed to perform R&D without additional supporting evidence" (ibid., p. 65). Consistent with the description of the design activity itself, the artistic work must also have research-relevant aspects in order to be regarded as R&D activity.

Phillips and Pugh (2005) described three areas in which research in design can be carried out: exploratory research, testing research, and problem-solving research. Exploratory research involves researching a topic or a theoretical or empirical problem that is still unknown, with the aim of discovering something new. Testing research is understood to be basic research with the aim of expanding existing knowledge about an area of generalisation. Finally, problem-solving research is understood to mean researching close-up problems with the aim of developing solutions using theories and methods, if necessary, from different disciplines. Both the qualitative and quantitative research process can be used in the three areas.

If one compares Phillips and Pugh's classification with the definitions from the *Frascati Manual* (OECD, 2015), exploratory research could be equated with experimental development, testing research with basic research, and problem-solving research with applied research.

B2   Learning by research

As universities strive to enhance the connection between research and teaching, forms of *learning by research* have become popular among university teachers, informing both course and curriculum design. Learning by research aims at students' engagement with elements of a research process, so that they experience how research is being conducted in their field of study (Huber, 2013, p. 9). Differing from other types of delivery, learning by research focuses on the process of generating knowledge, less than on conveying state-of-the-art research results in the respective field (Huber, 2014, p. 23). Key elements of learning by research are that students acquire the skills to organise their learning in an autonomous fashion, manage complex situations involving a multitude of factors, and deal with uncertainty. Thus, learning by research not only fosters discipline-specific knowledge and methods but promotes the acquisition of general competences, for example, analytical skills needed for generating one's own subject matter and devising a course of action (Mooraj & Pape, 2015, p. 2).

> "For the most important thing regarding learning by research as principle is the cognitive, emotional and social experience of the entire cycle that spans from curiosity or initial concern to the questions and structuring tasks of the outset over the highs and lows of the process, feelings of happiness and uncertainties up to the self-acquired insights or solutions to problems and the communicating of which" (transl. AR, Huber, 2013, p. 12).

Reviewing the literature on learning by research, we find a diversity of terms used, which leads to a considerable degree of ambiguity in the discussions and constitutes one of the main criticisms associated with this approach

(Deignan, 2009, p. 14). The differences in terminology point to varyious underlying concepts. Thus, in the following section, we will review the main concepts and then assess different strengths and challenges associated with learning by research.

Healey and Jenkins (2009) have put forth a typology of learning by research that is differentiated according to the degree of active student participation as well as the focus on research content or on the research process. The authors argue that enabling undergraduate students to participate in a research process which resembles the research processes academic staff embark on, is the most promising way to strengthen the nexus between research and teaching in universities. They make the case for the active involvement of undergraduate students as producers of knowledge from an early stage on – which should also be anchored in the curriculum. There is debate on whether the emphasis should lie upon the production of new knowledge relevant for the field, the possibility of which some contest for undergraduate work, or rather on the learning that is initiated through these processes (ibid., pp. 3, 6-7, 22-23).

Healey and Jenkins found four types of student engagement in research: "research-led: learning about current research in the discipline; research-oriented: developing research skills and techniques; research-based: undertaking research and inquiry; research-tutored: engaging in research discussions" (ibid., p. 6).

They claim that all four types of learning equip students with different types of relevant knowledge and competences and should hence be included in undergraduate courses and curricula to some degree. While research-led and research-oriented learning do not necessarily require active student participation, research-tutored and research-based learning necessitate didactic concepts that enable students to recreate some elements of a typical research process in the respective discipline (ibid., p. 7). Since "[t]he four ways of engaging students with research and inquiry are, of course, not independent", "[t]he way the four approaches are interlinked together is critical in the design of effective courses and programmes" (ibid., p. 8).

For the German-speaking area, Huber (2014) put forth a widely adopted typology, defining learning by research (*forschendes Lernen*), research-oriented (*forschungsorientiertes Lernen*), and research-based learning (*forschungsbasiertes Lernen*). The three concepts can be differentiated according to the elements of a prototypical research process with which they deal.

Research-based learning enables students to understand how general questions are transformed into research, what distinguishes scientific inquiry from everyday assessment of problems, and what constitutes scientific knowledge. Thus, it focuses on the beginning of a prototypical research process: defining the research problem, formulating the research question, etc. (ibid., p. 24).

21   Comparing positions

Research-oriented learning aims to equip students with the abilities to embark on a research process, thereby dealing with research methods, for example, how they are conducted and on what grounds they are selected (ibid., pp. 24-25).

Learning by research according to Huber means that students go through the main stages or even an entire research process, as is typical in the respective discipline. Students may work on their own, in teams, or participate in a larger research project in a meaningful way. This amounts to an initiation into a disciplinary "community of practice" (ibid., p. 25).

As Rueß, Gess, and Deicke (2016) have noted, both Healey and Jenkins' typology as well as that of Huber differentiate between learning formats according to the degree of active participation of students. Furthermore, they make a distinction between formats focused on the research content as opposed to those focused on the process as such. With the addition of research-oriented learning, Huber also creates one category revolving around research methods (ibid., p. 26).

Rueß, Gess, and Deicke also determined the dimension of student participation through an empirical study, concluding that student engagement may be viewed as reception, application, or research. For example, research-based learning (according to Healey and Jenkins) can take place in the form of learning about the stages of a research process through teacher instruction (reception). It may also take the form of students outlining and discussing a possible research project (application), or it can involve the autonomous elaboration of a research question and taking steps to answer that question (research) (ibid., p. 35).

While these typologies are helpful in systematising the subject matter and may also be usefel in an instructive manner for communicating with students, teaching practices in individual courses usually combine several of the abovementioned types (Huber, 2014, p. 28).

Dürnberger (2014) has argued that real-life learning scenarios typically fail to correspond to these analytical types. Thus, she prefers to think of the elements constituting learning by research as existing on a continuum, for example, between students as passive recipients and active contributors. In order to describe specific learning settings, she has devised the following model (ibid., pp. 37-39):

Continuum 1:	Predefined problem	►	Self-chosen problem
Continuum 2:	New knowledge for the student	►	Genuinely new knowledge
Continuum 3:	Learner-centered to a low degree	►	Learner-centered to a high degree
Continuum 4:	Low self-organizing	►	High self-organizing
Continuum 5:	Low social contextualizing	►	High social contextualizing
Continuum 6:	Low critical-reflexive analysis	►	High critical-reflexive analysis

Table 1: Learning by research continuum (Dürnberger, 2015; transl. AR)

In a similar vein, Brew (2013) has identified a lack of currently existing models and typologies for classifying learning arrangements – especially if they are to inform decision-making both on the course and on the curriculum level (ibid., p. 612). She proposes "a wholistic model for research-based learning decision-making", (see Figure 1). With this model, both teachers and curriculum designers can analyse the relevant aspects for developing learning by research, but also inquire into existing practices (ibid., pp. 612, 615).

Decisions may focus on what the learning outcomes are, what type of knowledge and skills shall be conveyed, and to what degree activities are pre-structured or autonomously decided on by students. This also extends to assessment. At the core of the model is a reflection on who the students of a particular course/curriculum are, what the institutional and disciplinary context is like, and which didactical approaches seem appropriate (ibid., pp. 613-614).

Learning by research provides distinct benefits for the students' learning experience. According to the literature analysed, these involve first and foremost forging a close link between teaching and research (Healey & Jenkins, 2009, p. 9). However, not only are research and teaching closely intertwined, but a strong connection is often established to knowledge and applications of specific working areas. The students' self-organising of the process and examination of the steps, methods, and knowledge gained contributes to deep-level learning, which makes it easier to transfer learnings to new fields of application (Huber, 2013, p. 16-18). Furthermore, learning by research enhances student motivation by encouraging self-study, thereby increasing student autonomy and active participation in the generation of knowledge (Mooraj & Pape, 2015, pp. 2, 6). Students who are not yet as 'disciplined' as academics with long years of academic training and instruction in the disciplinary ways of working are likely to take a new approach to procedures and do things differently than is usually done, thereby helping to innovate research practices (Healey & Jenkins, 2009, p. 9).

Since learning by research requires active student engagement (Dürnberger, 2014, p. 7), it facilitates a less hierarchical style of teaching and learning and encourages collaboration among teachers and students. This more active role of students enhances their identification with the discipline they are studying (Mooraj & Pape, 2015, pp. 6-7).

It is also more suited to accommodating student diversity, in terms of personal characteristics as well as regarding different types of learning, than more traditional forms of teaching. This is due to the fact that students have greater autonomy in choosing their style of work and in approaching the subject matter (Healey & Jenkins, 2009, pp. 38-39).

Consequently, students acquire specific types of skills in this learning format. Dürnberger, for example, claims that learning by research which takes place over the course of composing a bachelor's thesis is uniquely suited to

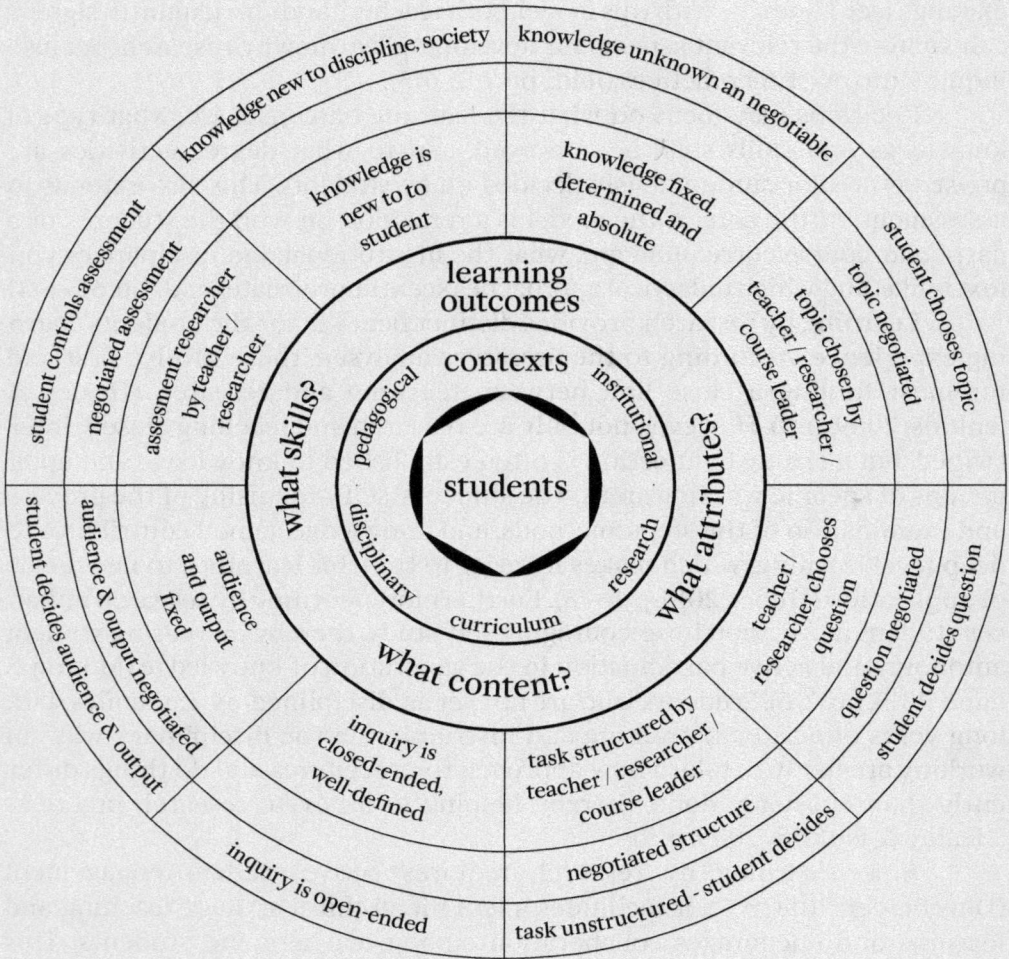

Figure 1: A wholistic model for research-based learning decision-making (Brew, 2013, p. 613)

advance key competences. This happens as a result of the openness of the process as well as the need for students to make autonomous decisions and take steps on their own to further their work. In this way, the development of key competences may be supported by the teachers with sound pedagogical approaches furthering learning by research (Dürnberger, 2014, pp. 1-2).

Among the skills learning by research is said to encourage, we find the ability to define a subject matter, formulate research questions and hypotheses, and envision a corresponding course of action to answer these questions in the reviewed literature (Mooraj & Pape, 2015, p. 2). Students learn how to structure a generally open work process, thus developing self-organising and time management skills, but also a competent handling of information: how to research, process, and assess (Dürnberger, 2014, pp. 64, 68-69). Learning by research also supports the development of reflective competences (Mooraj & Pape, 2015, p. 2) as well as the training of a critical attitude, to pose questions, deal with uncertainty, and consistently examine what is known (Huber, 2014, p. 23). In this way, students are enabled to critically assess what they are learning. Additionally, learning by research facilitates the transfer of general knowledge to a specific problem or field of application. It goes along with the development of a problem-solving mindset (Dürnberger, 2014, pp. 7, 64).

When listing the many pros associated with this learning format, we also need to mention the challenges that go along with it – both for teachers and for students. In the reviewed literature, we found that learning by research requires carefully thought-out didactic approaches. For example, in order to facilitate student engagement (initiate debates, reflection, the autonomous search for sources), a frontal style of teaching might suffice. However, pedagogic approaches that get students interested in participating in discussions, student projects, and excursions will become necessary (Huber, 2014, p. 24). In this way, learning by research is time-consuming for teachers (Riewerts et al., 2018, p. 399) as well as more difficult to schedule beforehand than more traditional teaching approaches (Mooraj & Pape, 2015, p. 7). Subsequently, the results of learning by research may not lend themselves to standardised ways of assessment which have to be conducted at universities (Huber, 2013, p. 22). Also, there are many decisions to be made here (see Figure 2): Which degree of openness or structure will be conducive to the type of learning that shall be achieved, etc. (Healey & Jenkins, 2009, pp. 67-78)?

For students, the process is also time-consuming. Some may also find it hard to deal with the open nature and the low degree of structure associated with this learning format (Mooraj & Pape, 2015, p. 7). Others who do not intend on proceeding with an academic career may deny that doing research has meaning for them and their future. This argument can be countered with the skills and key competences that are acquired through learning by research which are not only useful for academics, but transferable to a diverse set of employment options (Healey & Jenkins, 2009, pp. 50, 73-78).

On an institutional level, the question remains where this type of learning shall be placed in the curriculum, and how it may be thoroughly implemented throughout a study programme. It may be difficult to cater to all its requirements in only one semester (Riewerts et al., 2018, p. 399). Depending on disciplinary specifics or departmental needs, the people in charge have to decide whether learning by research may take place as an extra-curricular activity, a requirement for all students, or for individual students only (Healey & Jenkins, 2009, pp. 67-78).

B3   Artistic-scientific research

Not only the field of design, but the arts in general have been grappling over the last few decades with the question of whether art-related practices generate knowledge, and whether some of these practices may be called research. This discourse revolves around the concepts of 'artistic research' or 'arts-based research'. A thourough discussion of these concepts exceeds the scope of this publication. At the same time, they are to be mentioned here since they often serve as reference points for considering how to conceptualise design research – especially when talking about design research at the PhD level.

The discussion on artistic or arts-based research has been accompanied, if not even driven to a certain extent, by large-scale transformation processes in the structure of university education (for example, the Bologna Process), but also regarding the funding of universities as well as art and design schools (Daxer, 2019, p. 152). Moreover, it is a testament to science critically examining the processes of its own making, uncovering that the production of knowledge is riddled with creativity and intuition – properties commonly associated with the arts. This in turn blurs the purported clear demarcation between research as belonging solely to the domain of science and art production as something completely different (Badura, Dubach & Haarmann, 2015, p. 9).

A very general definition is given by Daxer: "Artistic research understands the artistic process itself as a procedure that generates insights and, as a consequence, knowledge" (transl. AR, 2019, p. 150). Yet reviewing the literature on artistic research, it can be stated that what it is, what it aims at, and how it can be conducted is heavily debated (ibid., p. 152). As a result, there are no commonly agreed upon standards for assessing artistic research and the quality of its outcomes (Badura, Dubach & Haarmann, 2015, p. 13).

As stated above, design positions itself at the interface between art and science. Thus, it cannot simply be considered one of 'the arts'. This becomes fairly obvious when one studies the various publications on artistic research. Design is either positioned as a discipline distinct from the others that the

26

publication talks about (for example, Mareis, 2010) or is touched upon only in a brief manner, while the major part of the contribution focuses on the fine arts. In this way, artistic research or arts-based research may be considered less relevant for developing research endeavours in design. Rather, these concepts may be considered as related, yet distinct approaches, dealing with similar questions, yet focusing on the (fine) arts, thus being unable to address the specifics of design and especially, in our case, product design.

B4   Forms of design research

Design as a profession has traditionally been associated with the applied arts rather than science. As the demands placed on this profession became increasingly complex and interdisciplinary, the aspect of research within this discipline was also found to have a certain degree of justification. Since then, there has been a lively discussion on the question of what design research is and which areas design research can cover.

The debate on what role research plays in design began as early as 1969 with Herbert Simon's claim that research in design offers a unique opportunity to think about new methods of knowledge production (Simon, 1996). Based on Bruce Archer's work and his call for design as a third area in design education in addition to the fields of science and humanities (Archer, 1979), Nigel Cross (1982) also deals with the question of knowledge production in design alongside the sciences and humanities. Apart from listing five types of knowledge production in design, which are "[d]esigners tackle 'ill-defined' problems, [t]heir mode of problem-solving is 'solution-focused', [t]heir mode of thinking is 'constructive', [t]hey use 'codes' that translate abstract requirements into concrete objects, [t]hey use these codes to both 'read' and 'write' in 'object languages'" (ibid., p. 226), he does not provide an answer to the question of how the implicit knowledge in design, the "designerly ways of knowing" (ibid., p. 223), can be made explicit.

In the early 1990s, Christopher Frayling published a definition of design research for the first time, suggesting a division into three areas: "Research into Art and Design", "Research through Art and Design", and "Research for Art and Design". The area of "Research into Art and Design" deals with historical, cultural, aesthetic, and perception research. "Research through Design" addresses the areas of material research, feasibility studies, and action research. And finally, "Research for Art and Design" includes reflections on the artefact that has been developed (Frayling, 1993).

Bruce Archer (1995) basically adopts Frayling's threefold classification but uses slightly different terms to talk about the relationship between a practitioner activity and a research activity. What Frayling calls "Research into Art and Design" is for Archer "Research for the purposes of practice" and falls into the categories of science or humanities and should be carried out according to the research standards of these disciplines. Frayling's category of "Research through Art and Design" is for Archer "Research through Practice", which both understand rather similarly, but Archer states that regardless of whether a material, process, or function is the focus of the investigation, research carried out in this category has to be conducted in the form of action research. Finally, Frayling's category of "Research for Art and Design" is called by Archer "Research about Practice" and is again similarly defined by its content, but Archer adds that research done in this category falls into the realm of the social sciences and should be conducted according to the discipline's standards (ibid.).

Findeli (1998) uses Frayling's definition to describe his point of view on the areas in which actual research in the context of design can happen. For Findeli, the research realm of "Research into Art and Design" is theory-oriented and makes no real contribution to a theory of design. Findeli understands "Research for Art and Design" to be practical applied science without theory and thus contributes nothing to the discipline. However, the area of "Research through Art and Design" has for Findeli the most potential of really contributing to a theory of design (ibid.).

Ken Friedmann (2003) advocates adapting design research to the standards of basic, applied, and clinical research. Wolfgang Jonas (2004), on the other hand, basically returns to Frayling's tripartite division of research in design, renaming Frayling's "Research into Art and Design" into "Research about Design" but essentially remaining true to the description that, for example, design theory or design philosophy is located in this area. Frayling's "Research through Art and Design" remains essentially the same in Jonas' "Research through Design", meaning the design's own research and design process. And finally, Frayling's "Research for Art and Design" remains "Research for Design" in Jonas' framework and is understood to refer to the research that later supports design. Researchers therefore provide knowledge through their work, such as research on user groups, market situations, etc., which makes a contribution to the success of the design.

In 2004, looking back on 40 years of design research, Nigan Bayazit argued that design research was divided into five areas. First, design research deals with the physical embodiment of artificial artefacts, how these artefacts do their work, and how they work. Second, design research is concerned with the creation of artefacts and the design activity of designers, how they work and think. Third, design research deals with the result of a targeted design activity and what it means. Fourth, design research deals with the formal aesthetic analysis of artefacts, and fifth, design research is carried out as a systematic search for knowledge and new insights that support design and drafting activities (Bayazit, 2004).

In 2009, Brandes, Erlhoff, and Schemmann referred to Frayling's division of design research into three areas, although they changed and expanded it by some aspects that Bayazit had already noted in 2004. The first sub-area, "Research into Design", includes research on design history and cultural studies, research on semiotics, market research, critical research, and ergonomics. The second area, "Research through Design", comprises material research, feasibility studies, ecology with regard to the use of materials, detailed analyses, and market and brand analyses. The third area is called "Research with and for Design" and differs significantly from Frayling's original description. Brandes, Erlhoff, and Schemmann understand research in this area as an examination of the sociality of design. This area is intended to examine design in terms of its importance for society and culture, using empirical social research (Brandes, Erlhoff & Schemmann 2009).

This book follows the definition set out by Brandes, Erlhoff, and Schemmann.

An examination of how the term research has been classified in the field of design over the last few decades shows that there seems to be a general consensus on three directions. Taking up the basic statements for each direction, an attempt is made to summarise the content as well as a discipline-specific combination:

► Research into design: can focus on historical and design-theoretical aspects and can be assigned to the discipline of the humanities.
► Research through design: can be conducted through material research and be assigned to the disciplines of engineering and natural sciences.
► Research with and for design: can focus on studying the users of arte-facts and can be assigned to the discipline of social sciences.

B5   Practice-based and practice-led research

After the chronological presentation of the changes in the definition of research in design, this subchapter will now deal in more detail with the practice-based research approach in design, which is often also used synonymously with the term research through design. The practice-based research approach is also not defined in a uniform way, since varyious definitions are used in different disciplines. This subchapter presents the concept put forth by Candy and Edmonds (2018) because it offers links to the typologies introduced above and can be easily connected to experiences of implementing learning by research into design education.

> "A basic principle of practice-based research is that not only is practice embedded in the research process but research questions arise from the process of practice, the answers to which are directed toward enlightening and enhancing practice" (ibid., p. 63).

"Stated simply, practice-based research is an original investigation undertaken in order to gain new knowledge, partly by means of practice and the outcomes of that practice" (ibid.).

The authors argue strongly against using the terms research and practice interchangeably, for the two are different entities with distinct qualities that may be combined in a meaningful way (ibid., pp. 63-64). Practice in the creative arts is directed at "the actual application or use of an idea, belief or method" (ibid., p. 64) in a way that transforms this item to generate something new. Usually, this transformation is thought of as some sort of creative process (ibid.). Research, on the other hand, means "systematic investigation to establish facts, test theories and reach new knowledge or new understandings" (ibid.) and must make a contribution that is shared and disseminated publicly (ibid.).

Candy and Edmonds distinguish practice-based research, in which "a creative artefact is the basis of the contribution to knowledge" (ibid.), from practice-led research, which generates "new understandings about practice" (ibid.).

"For practice-based researchers, making an artefact is pivotal, and the insights from making, reflecting and evaluating may be fed back directly into the artefact itself. Practice-led research, on the other hand, does not depend upon the creation of an artefact but is nevertheless founded in practice" (ibid., p. 65).

They develop their theory against the backdrop of PhD study programmes, in which the making of creative works is relevant to the degree itself – along with a written doctoral thesis (ibid.).

"[...] the creative works cannot be expected to speak for themselves in the context of a PhD submission. For that reason, they should, indeed must, be accompanied by some form of textual analysis or explanation to support the candidate's position and to demonstrate critical reflection" (ibid.).

The research not only demonstrates that students know how to use existing sources and discipline-specific research methods, but it grounds the works within the field, assessing their contribution, but also demonstrating their degree of novelty (ibid.). The written part of the thesis cannot stand alone either, making the question of how to relate object to text a central aspect of reflection (Candy, 2006, p. 1) – for students, teachers, and study programme developers.

Based on their many years of supervising students with practice-based PhD theses, Candy and Edmonds conclude that research in the creative arts does not match ideas of knowledge creation that follow a typical research process in the sciences. Rather, both the practice and the research process revolve around making a creative object. Yet at the same time, the research aspect of the project must be taken seriously in order to qualify as practice-based

30

research. That means writing about the context of the object as well as its contribution to the discipline or benefits it may provide to public audiences (Candy & Edmonds, 2018, p. 68).

Scrivener (2002) makes the general argument that research may be conceptualised slightly different in the creative arts (visual arts) than in the sciences, questioning the adequacy of having to generate new knowledge. Since within the creative arts, the production of an artefact and the creative process are at heart, they should also be at the centre of the accompanying research process. Thus, "the art making process is understood as a form of research and the art object as a form of knowledge" (ibid.), the art object even being the main result of the research process in his view. The role of the textual contribution to the artefacts produced would then be to justify this object and to communicate about its context, its contribution, etc. (ibid.) While this position remains open for debate at the PhD level, it can be instructive for constructing requirements at the bachelor's and master's level.

Vaughan, on the other hand, generally questions the validity of separating the results created in design study programmes from 'traditional' scientific outputs. As she argues, there is not one single version of a PhD (or, in the same way, a master's or a bachelor's) thesis, but they are always bound by discipline-specific standards as well as rules laid down by the institution awarding the degree (Vaughan, 2019a, p. 112). Thus, the reflection on the style and shape of the final products should happen with regard to design in its own right, "knowing when to use design to re-present the research and when to use text to discuss or describe the research" (ibid., p. 118).

B6   Conduction of research

In the context of the practice-led PhD research in the field of art, design, and architecture, Michael Hohl (2020) advocates orienting one's own work to the research habitus of established disciplines. The creative practice and reflected action in artistic research require the use of appropriate modes of action in order to make the implicit knowledge used in the artistic activity explicit.

Just as the definition of design research and its sub-areas has changed over the years, so has the method catalogue applied within this area. However, the reference to the processes and methods of social science research has remained the same. A variety of literature sources for conducting design research have emerged over the past decades. The concept of Muratovski (2016) is explained here in more detail because the publication specifically addresses designers.

Before any creative action is taken, a research problem needs to be defined to establish a sound, data-based foundation. It should be noted that questions concerning the function or construction of objects, data comparison without an underlying question, and examinations that would only output a yes or no answer are excluded as research problems. Basic knowledge of the field to be worked on should be available before any design research is carried out. After a research problem has been defined, the goal of the research project should be defined based on a research question. A comparative literature analysis, such as a chronological examination, historical research, thematic analysis, methodological comparison, theoretical comparison, or a meta-analysis, should provide an overview of the current state-of-the-art of research. Concerning the selection of a suitable research methodology, there are basically four methods frequently used in the area of design. The first and most frequently used is the qualitative research methodology. It examines how individuals experience their world in a certain context. The second is the quantitative research methodology, which is used to ascertain, for example, how an existing product is reflected and evaluated. The third method consists of visual research or material analysis and means the examination and comparison of objects or media created by humans. And finally, the fourth is applied research, which offers an opportunity to examine and reflect on one's own creative work. In design, this form of research is described as practice-based research. The research question determines the choice of research methodology. It should also be pointed out that a research study can also be carried out using a mixed-method approach, for example, a combination of qualitative and quantitative research methodologies (ibid., pp. 28 - 40).

B7   Standards of design research

Building on the definition of research as well as the different forms of design research presented above, the question arises as to which standards apply for design research, for example, practice-based design research, in order for it to be classified as research. Researchers around the globe are working towards specifying and outlining such criteria, yet to this date the debates still oscillate between the very divergent poles of striving to establish scientific standards, likened to standards in other disciplines with a longer history of being anchored in scholarly tradition, versus upholding the value of artistic knowledge that transcends common standards of scientificity.

Clemente, Tschimmel, and Pombo (2020) argue that design research, despite the extensive work over the last decades, has not yet been consolidated, thus impacting negatively on its own significance (ibid., p. 147). They cite Cash (2018) who speaks of a "lack of methdological development, validation and standardisation" (ibid., pp. 97 as cited in Clemente, Tschimmel & Pombo, 2020, p. 147), which prevents the results from being picked up by other disciplines. The authors maintain that design research has to produce "new communicable and explicit knowledge" that "follows rigorous scientific standards" (ibid., p. 150).

Tacit knowledge which may be generated through designing must be made accessible through reflection and lead to communicable results (ibid.).

Practice-based or practice-led design research is especially tied up with these ongoing debates since knowledge is created through practical designing and must be relevant for it. Prochner and Godin (2022) point to the specific nature of knowledge produced by design practice which may not always lend itself to being held to all the common standards of what is considered good research. At the same time, they note that so far "no consensus is found about how to evaluate the quality of RTD [research through design, AR] projects and their outcomes" (ibid.). This "forces researchers to rely on intuition rather than explicit guidelines when planning their work" (ibid.).

The authors refer to the many existing proposals for standards to hold practice-based design research accountable. They cite, for example, "a traceable process (Brandt & Binder, 2007), novel and defensible results (Höök & Löwgren, 2012), and contributions to theory and practice (Krogh & Koskinen, 2020)" (ibid.) Based on the dilemma of needing standards to assess the quality of design research projects and the objections to simply translating criteria from other disciplines to design, Prochner and Godin have devised a framework of quality indicators they think matches the characteristics of practice-based design research. The framework encompasses the dimensions of traceability, interconnectivity, applicability, impartiality, and reasonableness (ibid.).

Herriott (2019), on the other hand, contends that practice-based research or research through design does not differ from a standard research process in such a way that it warrants a distinctly new research process methodology (ibid., pp. 6-8), making way for the argument that this type of research can also be held to common criteria of what is good research.

B8   Relationship of the research definitions to the schemes

Returning to the original question of the chapter, i.e., what is considered research in design, it can be stated that the variety of approaches illustrated as well as the discussion about the establishment of standards for design research also explains the lively and controversial discussion about it. After attempting to compare the research definitions and schemes presented above, it is still not possible to give a generally valid answer to the question of how research in design is defined and what is actually recognised as research in design.

The reference in the *Frascati Manual* that higher education institutions should set research standards that also correspond to the established standards for research and development is taken up here and, despite the serious differences, this subchapter attempts to find common ground between the positions presented above.

Since this book deals with the implementation of research in product design practice, the way in which the conduction of research in design is understood is rooted in the field of constructive design research due to its premise that design research should be based on design practice and should be relevant for practitioners with regard to knowledge generation methods, processes, and aesthetic quality. Koskinen and Krogh (2015) stated that "[i]f design research can attract the curiosity and respect of design practitioners, it can alter their profession by encouraging informed, well-articulated, qualified interventions that fulfil the purpose of discussing design issues through creating concrete design objects" (ibid., p. 122).

In summary, it can be observed that, according to the definition given in the *Frascati Manual* and the abovementioned exclusion criteria for design research, as well as in the overview of the definitions of practice-based research, the artistic expression or the designed object itself is not considered to be research work. Rather, research work in design should take place through its contextualisation and further reflection.

Following the general understanding of scientific research described in chapter B.1, the forms of design research presented in chapter B.4, and the overview of definitions of practice-based and practice-led research in chapter B.5, a hypothesis on the relationship between these research systems is presented in Table 2.

basic research	◄ ►	research into design
applied research / practice-led research	◄ ►	research with and for design
experimental development / practice-based research	◄ ►	research through design

Table 2: Overview of the relationship between the definitions and the research schemes

Basic research is assigned to the area of "research into design". Without a specific field of application, a certain theory is assumed which is to be checked for validity. Due to the complexity and the required work experience within this research process, the research subject would represent, for example, the development of either a new theory model, a new technology, or a new material. This area is excluded at the BA level.

As a conclusion and working hypothesis, the concept of practice-led research is assigned to the definition of applied research as described in the *Frascati Manual*. Furthermore, applied research / practice-led research is identified as "research with and for design" because, in contrast to basic research, the central element here is the investigation of the practical translatability of a specific theoretical approach into design practice, such as the study of the users of artefacts. With reference to the question of compliance with discipline-specific research standards, the social science research methodology is proposed.

The experimental development research activity is assigned to the concept of practice-based research, which represents "research through design". The scientific experiment is defined as an empirical investigation in which specific conditions are created and their effects are observed (Flick, 2009, p. 308) and thereby hits the core of the area "research through design" with regard to, for example, the implementation of material research or feasibility studies.

In order to answer the main question of how practice-based research can generate new knowledge that can be recognised by scientific standards, a hypothesis for the research process, study design, and method selection for research projects in the field of applied research or practice-led research and research with and for design and experimental development or practice-based research and research through design will be presented in Part III of this book. The area of basic research was excluded for application at the BA level. ◄

C   Overall assessment of research in undergraduate design education

The next step is to assess the state-of-the-art of integrating design research into design education by systematically comparing existing approaches in different design study programmes. In a systematic literature review, we examined more than 80 articles, books, and online sources on the subject, aiming to analyse how to best forge the nexus between research, teaching, and design practice at the BA level. The discussion remains largely at the PhD level and only seldomly addresses design teaching at the undergraduate level. Almendra and Ferreira (2020) have identified this lack as a severe problem, arguing that "it makes no sense to have three cycles that are hermetically closed, for example, a practice-based intensive undergraduate course, a middle stage Masters which at the moment is more a continuation of the undergraduate than an effective pivot between design practice and design research, and a completely research-intensive PhD" (ibid., p. 199). Rather, basic design research skills should already be conveyed in undergraduate design study classes in an active way, meaning that students come to use them in their own projects (ibid.).

Candy and Edmonds (2018) put forth the concept of practice-based research and apply it to PhD programmes, which they then describe as practice-based PhD programmes. There are two main requirements students need to meet in order to graduate from such a programme. First, a creative object is produced that will be assessed. Second, the students need to contribute to the knowledge production in the disciplinary field in a substantial way – and this must happen in written form. The authors nevertheless concede that this latter requirement, which is a general requirement for all PhD programmes, may be formulated in a distinct way according to the specifics of creative disciplines (ibid., pp. 65-66). Knowledge that is generated within a practice-based research process in the creative arts may be:

> "understandings about audience experience, strategies for designing engaging art systems, taxonomies of emergent behavior and models of collaboration, to take a few examples. And of course, there are the works themselves: the artifacts, the compositions, the performances, the exhibitions and installations" (ibid., p. 66).

What remains open to debate is how the artefact and other research results are connected and how the latter is communicated in the best way possible (ibid., pp. 66-67). "Projects are vehicles for speculation through designing. Written work, whether it is a thesis or the exegetical component of a project, enables language-based speculation. Either mode of speculative undertaking may comment on the other, illustrate, amplify, or explain it" (Downton, 2012, p. 126).

Tonkinwise and Vaughan (2013) have proposed different types of written material that may qualify as relevant forms of communicating the research conducted, in addition to the tangible result of the creative practice:

> "These can be distinguished by when they occur: a) research reports of contextual inquiries produced prior to comprehensive designing that brief the design process b) reflective practice reports produced during, or based upon notes taken during, designing c) exegeses produced after the designing, locating the significance of the outcome or...
> They can be distinguished by their nature: 1. Social research (a or b) 2. Cultural theory (a or c) 3. Action theories of designing (b or c)" (ibid., p. 16).

Candy and Edmonds have argued that the research process may follow a distinct structure that is best specified within university examination rules (Candy & Edmonds, 2018, p. 66).

Much of the reviewed literature deals with PhD programmes – owing to the fact that in the last decades, more and more PhD programmes have been created in this field (Vaughan, 2019b, p. 5; Vaughan & Morrison, 2014, p. 3). The creation of practice-based PhDs has even been substantially supported by grants (Blythe & Stamm, 2019, p. 53; Dalton, Simmons & Triggs, 2019, p. 65). Moreover, conducting original research and thereby contributing to one's discipline is a requirement for PhD graduates in general, since a PhD qualifies students to pursue an academic career, which may also explain why there is so much debate focused on this study level. There is ongoing discussion on how best to compose a PhD curriculum in design (Tonkinwise & Vaughan, 2013; Vaughan & Morisson, 2013), which exceeds the scope of this review but builds the backdrop against which the current arguments revolve.

Coming back to the question of how best to integrate research in design project work, there are few authors who report on how they design their classes, which approaches and methods they use for teaching, and even fewer that deal explicitly with their efforts to help students build an active knowledge bridge between practice and research. One exception is Bruce M. Hanington (2010), who talks about a model of instructing students on design research methods at Carnegie Mellon University. The author presents a model that has been successfully used mainly at the MA level, but also sometimes at the undergraduate level, in human-centered design courses. He stresses that students must be introduced to research methods and doing research in a way that is linked with their creative process as designers, not only taking research classes in other disciplines, but connecting it to their projects (ibid., pp. 21-22).

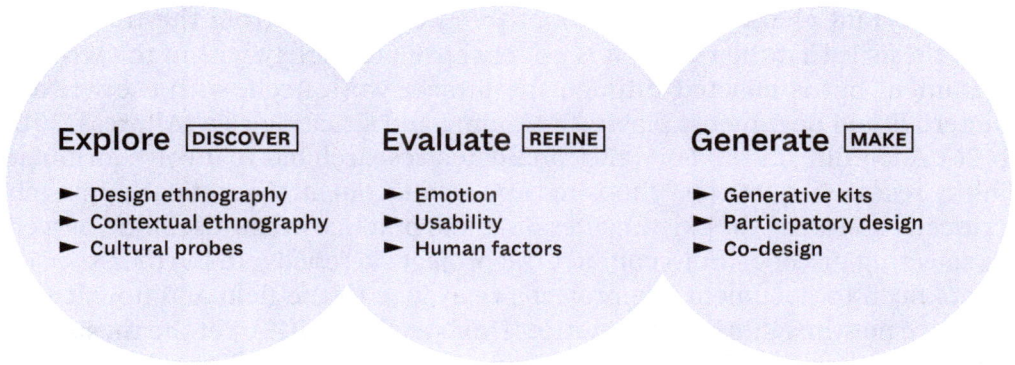

Explore `DISCOVER`
- ► Design ethnography
- ► Contextual ethnography
- ► Cultural probes

Evaluate `REFINE`
- ► Emotion
- ► Usability
- ► Human factors

Generate `MAKE`
- ► Generative kits
- ► Participatory design
- ► Co-design

Figure 2: Hanington's model for an active knowledge bridge between practice and research (2010, p. 21)

At Carnegie Mellon University, methods for "exploratory research", "generative research", and "evaluative research" are being taught in a process-oriented model (Hanington, 2010, pp. 21-25). Hanington argues for implementing research-based courses that are tied to studio projects into BA design curricula, since "undergraduate students also should have required courses and project work in research methods" (ibid., p. 25).

In the following, we will present approaches by RMIT University in Australia (Allpress et al., 2012), the National Research School in Sweden (Ehn & Ullmark, 2019), and AUT University in New Zealand (De Freitas 2002, 2007) for implementing some elements of an active knowledge bridge between design research and education. Their approaches differ with regard to how the artefacts produced are related to text and how the written elements of the thesis are understood.

At RMIT University in Melbourne, Australia, practice-led research has been implemented for all design study programmes at the master's and PhD level. The students work on their thesis project. In addition to the artworks they create, students are expected to write a justification of around 40,000 words and relevant models, images, or the like. The objects produced are exhibited and judged by a panel of experts, together with the written thesis. Design students even need to defend their work to the panel (Allpress et al., 2012, p. 2-3). The design objects are documented visually in the form of a Durable Visual Record (DVR) and the defences are videotaped. Everything is archived in the university library. The students are given the opportunity to take part in a mock exhibition and defence beforehand (Allpress, 2012, p. 26). "The strategies employed to supervise project-based methodologies and approaches support research outcomes relevant to these specific fields of practice that could not be achieved readily by other means" (Allpress et al., 2012, p.2).

An important characteristic distinguishing this model from the traditional PhD thesis is that the research is not encapsulated solely within the written document but is enacted through the project work itself, with the written materials and documents playing a framing and situating role (Allpress, 2012, p. 26). According to Duxbury, the candidates' research has to involve formulating a research question, choosing and laying out a theoretical approach, critically assessing the existing literature and practice in the discipline, as well as selecting methods fit to conduct the project sketched out. Further, the students need to document the project's relevance to the field and how it will produce new insights into the matter (Duxbury, 2012, p. 19). Yet the thesis also has to relate to the objects created in a way that includes documenting and interrogating the different stages of the project and reflecting on the creative practice throughout the study programme. What is important, though, is that the written thesis does not have to emulate a more traditional PhD thesis, since the students also perform creative work (Allpress, 2012, p.26).

Another key element of the RMIT model is that the supervisory process is structured around face-to-face meetings between students and supervisors, studio time, and the Practice Research Symposium, which takes place twice a year. Aside from students and staff, external experts are invited to discuss and review students' work in one-hour sessions. According to the stage of work the students are in, they present research questions, methods used, progress on their design process etc. In this setting, they not only receive input from academics or practitioners in the field, but they can also train how to best present and speak about their work (ibid., p.29). This ensures that the students not only feel part of a greater community of practice, but also of research and academia. Furthermore, it prevents students from working in isolation for the better part of their degree programme (Blythe & Stamm, 2019, p. 54).

Ehn and Ullmark (2019) call their approach "research education as co-design" (ibid., p. 83), which has been put to use in Sweden in the context of D!, the National Research School in Design. Following Schön (1983, 1987), the authors envision a "reflective practicum" (Ehn & Ullmark, 2019, p. 78) as a space for "learning-by-doing, coaching rather than teaching, and as a dialogue of reciprocal reflection-in-action between teacher and student" (ibid., pp. 78-79). This reflective practicum then builds the corner stone of their educational model. In contrast to Schön, Ehn and Ullmark do not remain focused solely on the design studio, but integrate PhD supervision, engagement with communities of practice and external experts, and course work into their model. The two-year programme is comprised of four meetings a year that range between two and three days in which students have to present at least once. Additionally, thematic courses are offered, and researchers are available for face-to-face supervisory meetings. Every second year, students are invited to the NORDES research conference, where they have the opportunity to present their work, and in-between they may participate in a summer school. In this way, PhD students are firmly integrated into the research community in the Nordic area (ibid., pp. 83-84).

Still, Ehn and Ullmark have identified several problems for educational practice, such as a lack of integration of students at their home universities and the low quality of PhD supervision due to the heavy workloads of their supervisors as well as inadequate expertise in the field of instruction (ibid., p. 84).

At the University of Applied Sciences in Potsdam, Germany, learning by research has been implemented university wide as a key strategy defining the university. The design faculty offers four study programmes: communication design, product design, interface design, and European media studies. In the following, we will describe how learning by research is approached in the first three design programmes, which are all practice-based degrees, oriented very much toward acquisition of job-related design skills. In this way, they are identified as well-suited for learning by research, since for the purpose of acquiring job-related competences, the curriculum supports students carrying out design processes in their entirety, from beginning to end (FL², 2015, pp. 4-5, 14). Both designing and researching require some of the same skills, for example, "the ability to solve complex tasks that can be planned only to a small degree and the composition of creative and innovative processes as well as communicating and cooperating in a team" (transl. AR, ibid., p. 14). There are several examples of how learning by research is implemented. For instance, project weeks are scheduled, which happen once a year and last for three weeks. Students have to participate at least twice during their studies. Courses are offered by all teachers in the different design programmes and students are free to choose, independently of their programme background. They spend the entire project week working on one question in interdisciplinary teams, reflecting on their work together at the end of the task, and exhibiting or presenting their results. The topics worked on transcend the usual programme content. Another example is the "project" module, in which students participate during the second part of their studies. In this module, students go through an entire design development process, often in cooperation with external partners (ibid., pp. 14-16). Research-related key competences that students acquire with this format of learning are "to observe, to research, to formulate a question, to create a concept, reflection" (transl. AR, ibid., 14).

The University of Applied Sciences also launched two projects to develop and promote learning by research at the institution. A number of initiatives were carried out, some of them involving design teachers and students. One example is the "Mobile Living" course that was held in 2014 and 2015, which focused on temporary living and working space and aimed to create an affordable assembly kit for that purpose. The course was conducted by teachers and attended by students from different disciplines, pursuing an interdisciplinary approach. The activities involved doing research into how the kit may be used – target groups, the bigger social, but also physical and legal context – as well as into creative practices, existing examples, and techniques. Based on their research activities, the students came up with ideas that were presented publicly with experts present. In the second semester, two prototypes were developed based on evolutionary prototyping, thus reflecting the students' diverse approaches. These prototypes were then further developed together with students so that they were ready for building and presented at two trade shows. In this context, learning by research was advanced in an interdisciplinary manner. Students were able to participate in an entire design process, starting with research and leading over to prototyping and development. Yet, students did not go through the entire process, but only participated in parts of the three-semester activity. Nevertheless, they were able to improve their methods skills and their ability to work and communicate in interdisciplinary teams. Additionally, the project supported the development of management and organisational skills (Prytula, 2016, pp. 81-85).

After conducting multiple courses integrating learning by research at the design faculty, the teachers involved concluded that in a one-semester course, one can either try to enable students to participate in an entire research process or focus on the training of specific research-related competences. Both have their merits but demand different course concepts. The authors stated that all research-related competences need continuous training and should be incorporated throughout the curriculum. At the same time, teachers should always encourage students to deal with ambiguity, even if they then fail, since trial and error constitute meaningful opportunities for learning (Langer & Schröder, 2016, pp. 144, 146-147).

In the debate on how to understand research and its connection to creative practice, De Freitas takes a firm standpoint, claiming that research starts from creative practice and revolves around it. "Practice-based projects in art, design and the performing arts can be defined as research even when they are not oriented towards an empirical world of data and information" (De Freitas, 2002). Yet they need to be properly documented (ibid.). De Freitas has described how practice-based research is documented in the Master of Art and Design Programme at AUT University, New Zealand. This is a two-year programme, in which the first year is concerned with courses and research, while in the second year, students perform project work in the studio. For a degree, students have to hand in a creative project and an exegesis of 3,000 to 6,000 words (ibid., 2007, p. 2).

A good exegesis situates the work in an appropriate context, discusses methods and theoretical orientations, identifies and discusses the problems encountered in the work, describes practical responses to those problems, and provides documentary evidence of the development or evolution of the work (ibid., 2002).

She has proposed "active documentation" (ibid.) as a research method through which ideas are generated, practice is reflected upon, and as a starting point for an exegesis (ibid.).

> "The term refers to a planned and strategic method of producing tangible visual, textual, or sound/video documentation of work in progress in such a way that normal studio practice is temporarily suspended, and it results in specific strategies being implemented. [...] Central to this method is the associated reflective practice, which can be described in this context as planned and deliberate activities that engage the artist or designer in a critical manner with the relationship between conceptual, theoretical, and practical concerns" (ibid.)

De Freitas surveyed students' perceptions of active documentation, interviewing arts and design students at AUT University (ibid.). She also tried to assess how the arts and design students document their work, how they connect the documentation to their creative practice, and their views on documentation in relation to designing (ibid., 2007, pp. 2-3). She found that the particularities of art and design research lie in "specific difficulties associated with the articulation of subjective dimensions and aesthetic judgements" (ibid., 2002). She called that a "complexity of overlap" (ibid.), the "tensions related to the balance and interconnectedness of analytical and creative components" (ibid.). As a result, students experience great difficulties in explaining "the way in which tacit knowledge of materials is acquired and used in practice, particularly in relation to aesthetic and emotive judgements" (ibid., 2007, p. 7).

Active documentation, for De Freitas, offers the means to do just that, a bridging of theory, practice, and the personal that may inform the students' learning experience as well as their ability to communicate their work (De Freitas, 2002; ibid., 2007, p. 7). Yet the interviews showed that many students fail to make a connection between documentation and reflection or analysis. A failure to establish a strong connection between these dimensions may lead to theses in which theory seems an odd add-on with little relation to methods and practical components (ibid., 2007, p. 7).

The results suggest that one particularly valuable aspect of active documentation is the way in which implicit and tacit details are extracted from studio processes. Active documentation appears to improve learning and to assist in the construction of meaning for the working artist/designer (ibid., p. 11).

Design education at the four institutions all present examples of implementing some sort of learning by research. Generally, reviewing the literature, it has to be stated that there are few sources which deal with the structure and the pedagogy of design education courses in a detailed manner. The ones that we found mostly deal with postgraduate studies (RMIT, D!, and AUT university). These programmes can be characterised by a heavy focus on individual student projects with which students acquire their degrees. For example, at AUT university, students spend an entire year in the studio, without doing additional course work. These postgraduate programmes are quite different in structure from undergraduate programmes which are characterised by ongoing course work and less time for students to focus on developing their final projects.

At AUT university, students have to compose an exegesis of 3,000 to 6,000 words, which aims at discussing theory and methods, but also documenting and situating the work. At RMIT, students need to develop a written thesis that is substantially larger in quantity and complies with 'traditional' research characteristics, such as formulating a research question, reviewing the relevant literature, developing a theoretical approach, etc. This points to different ideas about how the research conducted looks like and is communicated. While De Freitas argues for active documentation as a research method that enables a connection of theory, practice, and the personal and serves as a starting point for the exegesis (De Freitas, 2002), the authors from RMIT do not propose one approach to research. It is only stated that research is practice-led (Allpress et al., 2012, p. 3) and that relevance to the discipline, novelty, and dissemination of results serve as criteria (Duxbury, 2012, p. 19).

One element of their models that is noted both by RMIT and Ehn and Ullmark is that students should become part of a community of practice – both of professionals and of researchers. This is to be achieved by inviting external experts and subjecting students to discussion and critique of their (on-going) work by these experts – through symposia or the like (Allpress, 2012, p. 29; Ehn & Ullmark, 2019, pp. 83-84).

The example of undergraduate design education that we offered remains even less specific with regards to modes of instruction, concepts of design research that are to be adopted by students, and details on how learning by research is implemented. Different initiatives of learning by research are presented, which focus on teamwork and interdisciplinarity (FL², 2015, pp. 14-16; Prytula, 2016, pp. 81-83). The aims of these initiatives lie in students developing key competences that are relevant for research as well as for design and may be easily transferred to future jobs (FL², 2015, pp. 4-5). The projects introduced are heavily influenced by teachers, for example, by determining the research topic and question or the course of action. From the reviewed literature, it is not clear whether students also carry out individual projects in which they themselves develop the question or issue. However, the information provided on the homepage of the study programmes suggests that students are also involved in individual design projects (Fachhochschule Potsdam, 2019).

One aspect that is hardly touched on at all is the question of assessing the thesis, the artefact created, and their relation. Dunin-Woyseth and Nilsson (2014) are strong advocates of design research not emulating research from other disciplines, but developing in its own right with specific approaches, methods, and criteria. They concede that

> "in order to achieve recognition for the results of this research among both practitioners and researchers of architecture (and other scholars), the principles for assessing this kind of research should be discussed in a broader debate between design practice and (design) academia" (ibid., p. 11).

In their view, assessment should always be carried out by practitioners in the field as well as academic scholars, with criteria derived from both realms (ibid.).

From the accounts of integrating research in design education, two main themes emerge: students' experiences of research-based design projects and teachers' experiences supervising these projects. Thus, in the following, we will deal first with the students' perspectives and then the teachers' experiences.

C1 Students' experiences of research-led design studies

In 2008, Hockey stated that there were hardly any studies on students' experiences of doing research in creative arts and design study programmes (ibid., p. 109). The author reported of a study in the UK, conducted between 1995 and 1997, in which 50 PhD students of art and design were interviewed on their experiences during studying. The study found that most interviewees had previously had little exposure to academic writing, since they had mostly graduated from practice-oriented or even practice-only master's programmes. Their self-image thus also revolved around being a creative individual and 'making' things (ibid., pp. 109-111). Hockey even went so far as to interpret the need to develop academic writing skills as "a reality 'shock' to their [the students', AR] artistic identity" (ibid., p. 111). Additionally, the amount of work necessary to perform research was perceived as threatening as well – and as imposing on the time which could be spent on the genuinely creative tasks. Moreover, Hockey reported that formal documents provided to students to structure and communicate their research were perceived as restrictive, limiting their creative process (ibid., p. 112).

Regardless of the type of project they were undertaking, eventually all the students encountered the problem of analytic documentation and recording of demonstrable evidence in some form or another. Whilst artists and designers have traditionally kept notepads and sketchbooks, the systematic reflexivity of practice required by formal research enquiry was a surprise to all the interviewees (ibid., pp. 111-112).

Depending on the type of project (subject, approach used, etc.), it was easier for some students to follow the requirements of systematic documentation and reflection than for others (ibid., p. 113). Interestingly, Hockey concluded that breaking away from the creative practice to engage in research and documentation activities was perceived as being especially problematic during a very productive creative phase, "for then analytical documentation constituted a distraction, a step backwards from being engaged with materials, objects and processes" (ibid.).

Hockey distinguished between three types of strategies students use to deal with the demands of doing research and documenting it in a structured and analytical way. One group of students had little interest in the research aspect of the PhD programme; they had taken it up in order to receive funding to further their creative practice. In this way, they only complied with research requirements at a minimum level in order not to lose the funding (ibid., p. 114). "So, delay, deception, and minimal research activity were tactics deployed within the general strategy [...]" (ibid.). A second type of strategy identified was to try to meet the challenges of combining creative practice and research by acquiring new skills needed. The students in this group reported having come to terms with the requirements through a rather difficult process – yet in a way that impacted negatively on their creative output. At the same time, they found new career opportunities owing to the acquisition of research skills (ibid., p. 115). Lastly, students who struggled to meet both demands of research and creative practice and succeeded, developed a self-view that incorporated being a researcher as well as a creative professional. They also identified some benefits of linking research and practice, which meant that the taking up of a research degree actually improved their creative practice (ibid., p. 116). "Once this realization was reached, students began to conceptualize research itself as a creative process, not just a mechanical or technical one, and similarities between their making and this new endeavour gradually became evident" (ibid.).

Duxbury (2012) described similar experiences from her supervisory practice. Students that embark on a practice-led research degree at RMIT University, Australia, generally "undergo a form of crisis and a period of self-doubt when they realise that their proposed project must be converted from one grounded in professional practice to one that meets the requirements of research" (ibid., p. 19). Furthermore, Allpress noticed, also at RMIT, that some students fear they will be asked to create a practice that is then argued for with a certain theory, justifying what is being done creatively. Since this is experienced as inhibiting, supervisors have to open up a room of reflection and contestation (Allpress, 2012, p. 37).

"Tussling with the complex, contested, and mutually informing relationship between discourse and design is an activity that all candidates need to undertake if they are to find their voice to better articulate and theorise their own practices, and to situate them critically against the field to which they are contributing" (ibid.).

Dunin-Woyseth and Nilsson (2014) conceded as well that embarking on a PhD and engaging with research led to a changed identity for many of their students, impacting also how they view their professional practice of designing. It tends to be more reflective afterwards, drawing from different subjects and areas of knowledge (ibid., p. 12).

Shreeve, Bailey, and Drew (2003) reported that in the British higher education context, design students have to perform some sort of research on a regular basis (ibid., p. 115). This "may involve finding out about aspects of existing user information, markets, analysis of the problem, and written and visual exploration in order to inform decisions" (ibid.), but also "[t]he development of individual 'ideas' and starting points for the form of the individual design response made about the final design" (ibid.). The authors found that the research undergraduate design students do differs quite substantially from research on a postgraduate, academic level. As a result, they surveyed undergraduate fashion design students' views on research. The study focused on the experiences of first-year and beginning of second-year students (ibid., pp. 115, 117-118).

Shreeve et al. found four types of approaches to research, which are summarised in Table 3.

Project	Strategy	Focus on	Intention
A	To find out about, collect, visual information	Visual, literal elements	To reproduce visual elements of research in product
B	To make visual comparisons	Visual, literal elements	To reproduce visual elements of research in product
C	To understand the phenomena researched	Understanding	To demonstrate the process of research in product
D	To construct own response through research	Conceptual, emotional, abstract elements	To convey own idea/concept in the product

Table 3: Approaches to research in the design project (A-D) described in terms of strategy and intention components (Shreeve et al., 2003, p. 125)

In the first approach (A), research is done in order to apply the ideas found to the appearance of the creative object, 'translating' them in a literal way (ibid., pp. 119-120). Similarly, in the second approach (B), students do research in order to "reproduce visual elements in the finished product" (ibid., p. 120), yet they do so by connecting elements of different sources and artists. In the third approach (C), the research "is geared towards constructing a personal understanding of the phenomena researched" (ibid., p. 121) and "use this understanding in the design process to develop a product, which conveys the essence of the topic researched" (ibid.). Unlike the first two, students pursuing this approach use the research as part of a communication process and form their own concepts through the processing of knowledge (ibid., pp. 121-122). The last approach (D) is described as "focused on an abstract, emotional and conceptual response to a theme or topic researched, with the intention to convey an idea or concept through the designed product" (ibid., p. 123). Not only are diverse sources used, but the creative work is seen as an element of the research process. Yet, students following this last approach may also adopt strategies from the other approaches, which are integrated into their more complex course of action (ibid.).

Shreeve et al. have argued that the adoption of a specific approach largely depends on the learning environment and cannot be interpreted as a student-specific attribute (ibid., p. 127). Thus, "students undertaking the design project might perceive the research component as requiring a formulaic response" (ibid.) if it is "not related to a personal interest or a need to construct meaning, or involve emotion and feeling" (ibid.). This may be due to students interpreting the research as not being meaningful for the end product, which is the students' main interest. If teachers wish to alter the approach taken, they have to convey an understanding of research and of its relevance to the students. Furthermore, Shreeve et al. stated that the approach taken directly influences the learning experience. Students adopting approach A will develop relevant competences to a lower degree than students embracing approach D (ibid., p. 127-128).

> "If we fail to explore with students the ways in which we expect them to undertake the research elements of project work, or if we ourselves hold certain expectations of research at odds with a student's way of approaching research we begin to build in failure to our learning situations. There are implications for assessment; [...] what do students perceive as the requirement for the research component in the assessed design project? Are we prepared to accept differences in the way research is carried out?" (ibid., p. 128).

C2   Experiences supervising practice-based design projects

Allpress et al. have criticised that little has been published on how to teach and instruct students doing practice-based research in design and other creative fields as well as on didactic approaches and methods (ibid., 2012, pp. 3-4).

Due to the wide variety of students' backgrounds (academic, professional, personal), "a one-size-fits-all approach to supervision is out of the question" (Duxbury, 2012, p. 17). Rather, the educator may have to perform a multitude of different functions "such as a director, facilitator, advisor, teacher, critic, supporter, collaborator, friend or mentor" (ibid.).

The supervisor's role is to reassure the candidate that the project can be adapted to address real-world research questions through valid aims and objectives that will produce outcomes not only meaningful to the candidate, but also accessible and relevant to the community. Quality supervision ensures that the candidate will be confident that the articulation of ideas through their practice as an artist is the research and has the potential to result in new knowledge (ibid., pp. 19-20).

Ehn and Ullmark used the metaphor of a travel guide:

> "We often regard this work as travelling with the PhD Student. We are not deciding where to go, but are expected to guide the tour so that important places and experiences are not missed, and also to point to the experiences of other people who have made corresponding tours [...]. At the same time, we have to remind the student of the limited time available, and actively ask for priorities to be considered" (Ehn & Ullmark, 2019, p. 85).

Duxbury proposed a couple of stages for supervising a practice-led research project in the creative arts (in a three-year degree programme). The first stage, which can be described as "negotiation" (Duxbury, 2012, p. 19), calls for a creative approach both on the part of the supervisor and the student and is full of conversations between the two. In this stage, the core of the project is defined, as well as the thematic focus and the direction it shall take. This involves that students spending a lot of time on their work, but also branching out and conducting research on how their topic is dealt with in different contexts and disciplines. This means that students need less time with their supervisor and more time to work on their own (ibid., pp. 19-20).

The making of art is a reflective activity that takes time – time to make mistakes, time to experiment with unfamiliar media perhaps, and time to engage in creative play. It is an important period for the candidate to regain their independence, collect their thoughts, and test out ideas without someone overseeing them or regularly checking in for meetings (ibid., p. 21).

In this stage, in which regular progress meetings are held between supervisor and student, Duxbury also argued for students exhibiting their work as often as they can, for this is a way of communicating it publicly, one requirement of doing research (ibid.). In addition, the author recommended "'hands on' supervisor[s]" (ibid.), who step in when they feel that a student is procrastinating or running into trouble.

In the stage of finalising the practice-led research project, more extensive guidance again becomes necessary. Duxbury argued that each part of the practice-based degree (the object created, the written justification, the exhibition, and the visual documentation of the object) needs distinct supervision and instruction on the part of the educator. She stated that especially the supervision of the written thesis often effects a change of role. In her view, teachers then need to be more directive, instructing the students with little experience in documenting research more firmly than during the process of creating, designing, and producing art (ibid., p. 22). "As a supervisor of the exegesis I am both content and copy editor, setting particular tasks for chapters, and requiring compliance regarding referencing, legibility and relevance" (ibid.). Even though the writing-up of the research should go hand-in-hand with the other activities over the course of the three-year programme, it is usually primarily done in the last year (ibid.).

Downton (2012) argued that within this process, the supervisor first helps students to broaden their horizon, to open-up their project and question not only what already exists (in design, in the literature, in different disciplines), but also their own approaches and modes of creation. At later stages then, the supervisor instructs the students to narrow their enquiry and to support and motivate them in what they are doing and what they have already created (ibid., p. 125).

In his view, the main activity students need help in is examining and reflecting on their own practice – a central dimension for establishing a connection between research and practice (ibid., pp. 125-126).

C3   Core learnings:
Towards research-based undergraduate design education

As outlined above, much of the literature reviewed focuses on the PhD level. Less attention is being placed on how to implement a link between research and practice at lower-level studies. Since this publication is intended to be instructive for courses taught at the bachelor's level, we have to take the experiences reported from PhD programmes and analyse in which way they may inform teaching practices for undergraduates.

According to Dürnberger (2014), bachelor's theses, even though they are very different in approach, scope, style, and formal requirements depending on the institution and the discipline, fulfil four different types of functions. They are directed at the synthesis of core study content in a way to create something new (research dimension) and to prove students' ability to produce, assess, and reflect on results with approaches and methods relevant to the discipline (examination dimension). The bachelor's thesis is the formal degree requirement (qualification dimension) and marks a transition to future contexts of employment (job preparation dimension). Dürnberger sees it as equivalent to the piece of work a crafts(wo)man produces in order to show their mastery and ability to work in the field (ibid., pp. 13-14). Thus, bachelor's theses also include the demand for research, yet to a lesser degree than PhD theses which are explicitly research degrees (Friedman, 2017, p. 515).

The process of composing a bachelor's thesis combines learning and research in a unique way. While learning involves an individual student acquiring new knowledge and competences, research stands for generating new ideas for an audience – the community of scholars, the community of practice, and society at large (Didion & Wiemer, 2009, p. 7). The aspect of individual learning and acquisition of competences is however primary and needs to be supported with sound didactical approaches by teachers and supervisors (Dürnberger, 2014, p. 21).

One point made by a teacher of a creative design subject as part of a survey on the teaching-research nexus is that undergraduate students tend to be preoccupied with learning the visual language of the field that they are studying. The mastery of that visual language seems primary, while verbal reflection and analysis is usually engaged in at the PhD level (Wareham & Trowler, 2007, p. 10).

Thus, for the implementation of research-based learning formats in design education at the undergraduate level, teachers and curriculum designers need to find answers to the following questions in order to be able to construct adequate models of teaching.

What is the aim of the undergraduate research conducted?
- ► Is it directed at producing new knowledge, and if so, in what way and for whom?
- ► Is it directed at students acquiring competences? Are they research-related competences, transferable key competences, or other competences (related to methods, specifics of the discipline, etc.)?
  - ► Which of these competences can students already build on and to what degree?
- ► How does the research relate to the design practice carried out?

What degree of mastery shall be demonstrated? For example, what are the competence levels that students have to meet?
- ► How is the acquisition of these competences to be demonstrated – both in the object(s) created and in the additional text/visual documentation?
- ► How will the competence level be assessed?

Which approach to research is taken, and how is its relevance for improving design practice best communicated to students?
What is the greater (institutional, disciplinary, curricular) context, and how does it shape the parameters of the course?

- ► How much time is available? Which facilities?
- ► Which institutional rules may impact on course design (for example, regarding formalised assessment or timelines)?
- ► Who are the students (previous knowledge, personal characteristics, professional/disciplinary background, etc.)?
- ► Which didactical approaches and supervisory styles may be best adopted?

An analysis of the scanty research we found on students' experiences of embarking on research-based design projects reveals there are a few aspects that have to be taken into consideration when planning a design course with learning by research – even though they may not be as pronounced among all students:

- ► Students often have little previous experience with academic writing
- ► Their identity as an artist/creative person collides with the demands of research
- ► Research takes time away from their artistic work
- ► The structure of research may be perceived as limiting the creative process
- ► Teachers need to show how the research improves creative practice and how it is itself a creative practice

It became clear that questions of supervision lie at the heart of implementing research-based design projects. Authors agree that supervisors have to perform a multitude of roles, depending on where the students are in the process and what they need. Supervision may involve being more directive at times and giving students a lot of independence at other times. It may even involve a more supportive relationship, in which the supervisor assures the students of the quality of their work. The most important aspect of supervision during research-based projects seems to be that teachers help to establish a connection between the research conducted and the creative practice. This includes facilitating and aiding the development of specific ways of reflecting on their practice and connecting it to theory, context, and conceptual considerations.

There is little research on pedagogy and didactics in the creative arts as a whole, and articles on the study of teaching and learning tend to omit these disciplines (Klebelsadel & Kornetsky, 2009, p. 103). While there is little on the study of teaching and learning in the creative arts, this field seems to be developing over the last couple of years, specifically in design research.

Indicative of this fact is, for example, the uptake of the issue by the CUMULUS conferences (see, for example, the conference in Rovaniemi in May 2019, which focused on the future of design teaching [CUMULUS International Association of Universities and Colleges of Art, Design and Media, 2019]).

Thus, there are only a handful of accounts on implementing research-based or research-led formats of teaching into design education. Most of them do not present specific models, but rather examples of different approaches to specific questions, for example, how to develop practice-based PhDs, how to supervise candidates, etc. What is lacking to date is a detailed process documentation of how links between research and design practice are established in study programmes or individual courses. ◄

D	RIDE project:
	Steps taken, trials and learnings

E	Main competences in a design process
	(phase 2)

Research Project

D RIDE project:
Steps taken, trials, and learnings

The "Research in Design Education: Artistic-Scientific Research in Design Teaching Practice" research project, in short "RIDE", was conducted at New Design University, St. Pölten, Austria from March 2019 to August 2022. In four successive phases, the topic of integrating design research in design practice in a BA level design study programme was tackled from different angles, leading up to the development of the guidelines presented in Part III of this publication.

In the first phase (phase 1), the project focused on assessing current concepts and models of research-based teaching in design education (such as learning by research or practice-based research) and analysing their strengths and weaknesses for an application at the BA level. Simultaneously, the existing practices of integrating research into student projects in two courses of the "Manual & Material Culture" bachelor's programme at New Design University were studied, identifying problems and working areas for integrating design research into students' practices.

The second stage (phase 2) built upon the preliminary result that there was no universally accepted process of a design-scientific way of working, thus requiring design educators to develop solutions for the need for research-based design work in design studio practice. In order to indentify the specifics issues that arise for research-based design teaching, a mixed-methods study was carried out, investigating core competences among design students and examining whether the required core competences within each individual phase of a design process might provide information about the problems in building bridges between design research and design practice.

The third stage of the project (phase 3) addressed the area of design research with regard to the specific profile of the "Manual & Material Culture" bachelor's programme, which, in addition to teaching design skills, also places high demands on implementation and material competence and requires craft skills from its students. Since this research area still lacks definition and process guidelines, the study aimed at investigating applied processes from designers with the aim of using the knowledge gained to set up a new guideline for it.

The last stage of the RIDE project (phase 4) involved compiling the findings in this publication as well as holding a symposium on "Teaching research in design", which took place on 24 June 2022.

D1   Starting point (phase 1)

In the "Manual & Material Culture" bachelor's programme at New Design University in Lower Austria, persons with a secondary school degree and a background in the crafts trades are admitted to study design. In the project-oriented teaching, craftsmanship and artistic as well as scientific working methods are applied. In the last term, as part of the practical bachelor's project, which is carried out in a design studio course, students are required to prove their ability to integrate design research into their practical projects. Based on the experience of the six years leading up to the RIDE project, students perceive input given on design research and their work in the design studio as separate entities. They do not apply the research methodology learned in the courses to their practical projects. Based on this observation, a qualitative case study was developed, focusing specifically on two courses of the study programme, the design practice-oriented course, design studio, and the design research-oriented course, Research Lab. The two courses are taken by students in the last semester of their BA to carry out their practical bachelor's thesis.

The main question of the study was "How can the work methodologies of design practice and design research courses in general be transformed and intertwined in design teaching at Bachelor level to build the necessary knowledge bridge between theory, empiricism, and design practice in research-led teaching?" The case study adopted a participative approach (Brandes & Schaefer, 2013), using research methods from the social sciences, namely participant observation, interviews, and document analysis. The main data upon which the following results are based are drawn from 30 consultations between students and supervisors and six problem-centered interviews with students.

In the following, we will show how students approached the task of carrying out a research-led bachelor's project, focusing on their efforts to combine a structured process methodology for grounding their project in research with a more open, artistic approach to designing and producing the final products. We will analyse how the two different modes of practice may benefit from each other and in which instances their linkage proves problematic. Furthermore, we will assess how the students used the proposed process methodology, closing with core learnings for future research-oriented design classes.

Even though the students felt confident that they had learned the most relevant aspects for carrying out a design process on their own, all the interviewees expressed problems when asked to combine scientific-methodological approaches with creative tasks. From a student's perspective, there were two main reasons for problems linking the different ways of working. One reason is that the two courses studied each focus on one working style. The other reason is general insecurity on the part of the students concerning how to translate what they identify as research into a specific design process.

D2 Linkage between the design studio and research-oriented course is lacking

The students interviewed saw both courses as relevant for their practical bachelor's project. Yet they questioned why the courses were so clearly separated from each other in terms of time and date as well as the contents discussed.

> "Well I think that, the idea itself, I like, but I think that there is still a lot of room for improvement. And in particular the two courses should go hand in hand to a greater extent, so that you don't feel like there is somehow something separate still to come which is the other big part, but that it is certainly one bachelor thesis" (student).[1]

In this example, a student wishes to be able to talk in both courses about practical issues and questions relating to design, construction, and the like. In the same courses, he would like to be able to discuss about theory. "Therefore, I believe if it were possible to combine the two, also the knowledge fields of theory and practice just then, that, in my mind, would be a great blending and, I believe, a very productive mix. Yes. As it is, I feel it to be a little disempowering" (student).

The students having written a theoretical bachelor's thesis in the fifth semester, the practical dimension of their bachelor's project is at the forefront in their last semester. To them, the research-oriented part was dealt with in the theoretical thesis and so they now turn their focus to designing an artefact. Thus, the research surrounding the artefact as well as the documentation and reflection on their artistic work is of lesser priority. "Am not yet immersed into theory, my head is still grappling with practical considerations, but I have the feeling that theory will come with that" (student).

Thus, students stated that they were fine with the proposed process methodology, yet they usually waited to write the relevant pieces until the very last days of the semester. Still, all of the students interviewed reported that they were used to documenting their work process from the beginning on. They were taking photos, for instance, or collecting literature sources and links.

Students dealt with the scientific-methodological approach to their final project throughout the semester in the design research-oriented course. The various elements of this course were helpful to students in different work stages. On a positive note, the students expressed that they received a lot of help in finding a research question and reflecting on their chosen topic. Moreover, they appreciated the literature tips they received from the instructor. In this way, students were encouraged to deal with the topic of research questions throughout the semester.

1 All translations of the students' statements are the authors' own.

Furthermore, students were offered lecture notes sketching out the process methodology, but also giving sources and how-to examples, like templates for user research. While some students appreciated the scope of the documents provided, others found them off-putting.

> "I don't like bulky scripts like that, they always feel threatening to me. Especially in instances when you do not have anything to show yet. But then there are so many possibilities and you should ... To be honest, I have not even taken a look inside the script yet. [...] But this script feels so heavy, I do not even know, whether I need the contents or if they are just there as basics. Thus it feels like ... a millstone that I do not even want to see yet" (student).

To the students, it was not clear how much weight should be put on the research-oriented course. While they all recognised the purpose of precisely documenting their work, some of the interviewees were opposed to providing an analytical treatment of their topic to the extent of a theoretical bachelor's thesis.

> "Well to me it is obviously important that for the practical bachelor project I will have a factual object, having written a theoretical paper for the theoretical bachelor thesis. Now I am doing more or less a documentation of my project, but I do not want a small theoretical bachelor thesis" (student).

Having to put equal emphasis on both courses and the tasks associated with each is experienced as challenging:

> "Especially with this scientific writing about design, I am quite soon at the end of my capacities, where I have to say, actually I would need to spend all my time on this task. In order to arrive at a good result, a good quality result, I would have to focus only and solely on working scientifically, so that I can cope with that. To manage both in the same quality is impossible based on my current competences. They have improved already, but I still find it almost impossible that both operate at the same level" (student).

Students need to possess a broad skill set in order to meet the demands of developing a research-oriented practical design project – in addition to designing and carrying out the practical project. They have to be able to find sources, to read and to extract what is relevant for their own work, and comply with the standards of scientific practice and referencing. Students are expected to carry out elements of applied research. In many instances, this means doing user research and interviewing members of the target group in order to discover their preferences as well as contexts and ways of application for the planned artefact. It may also involve experimenting with materials, doing research graphically, or other forms of inspiration on different levels. What is more, they need to be able to document the progress of their work in both visual and textual form. Writing a scientific text further involves the skill of structuring the text. In the students' study programme, the structure of the final thesis was prescribed by the project documentation template.

The students interviewed had a number of ideas on how to improve the link between the course on research and the studio. First of all, it was recommended that the classes take place on the same day, and at least in some instances at the same time with both instructors present. In that way, students would receive feedback from the perspectives of all the teachers involved.

In the opinion of one interviewee, all students should align the theoretical bachelor's thesis, which is written in the fifth semester, with the practical bachelor's project, which is carried out in the sixth semester. Both pieces of work should be done in the same field, meaning that one topic is chosen both for the theoretical and the practical thesis. In this way, research and design practice could be better interrelated. "In order for it to forge one ensemble which fits" (student).

Another student, who had big difficulties finding a topic for their practical project, proposed something similar. In their experience, at the beginning of the sixth semester students were still concerned with the theoretical thesis. Thus, it would be helpful if the choosing of a topic was moved up to the beginning of the fifth semester. This would benefit not only the discussion of research, but also working on a final object.

> "It would be good if you had the time to really, extremely learn the ropes scientifically in a specific area and to then be able to put that into practice, because you probably won't have the time to do so in everyday working life. I see potential in that, then you would probably understand well why research is important for designing objects or just well ... yes. [...] But I think that that would be cool and then you would not have the forced alignment in the sixth semester, because that would have already been covered" (student).

D3 Students were unsure how to integrate design research into their specific practical design project

While the students had some ideas on how to combine research and design practice on an abstract level, most of them seemed at a loss when it came to talking about their specific project. The reasons stated ranged from the theoretical and practical bachelor's theses being conceived as distinct, unrelated entities to their own levels of competence to the nature of some projects being unsuitable for the integration of design research.

On a general level, the students considered design research to be highly beneficial for producing a high-quality design project. Yet when asked about their own bachelor's projects, they failed to see the merits of integrating research. Three interviewees expressed the opinion that their projects really did not need design research perspectives. This feeling hinged upon a lack of ability to personalise their notion of what research is. Research and research-related activities seemed fine when carried out for their sake, but they did not have a bearing on conceiving, designing, and constructing an artefact. Other interviewees happily integrated aspects of design research into their practical project – because they identified specific benefits in doing so. One student, for instance, reported that discussing his designs with members of the target group helped him to make design-related decisions on how the final versions should look.

If the students did not see specific benefits of integrating design research into their practical bachelor's project, they tended to be opposed to that requirement. A more formulaic notion of design research and working in a research-oriented way impacted negatively on the students' progress on the work. Yet it must be clearly stated that a successful blending of design research and practice was also based on the students' skills. Another factor impacting negatively on the link between research and practice was a shortage of time.

What did the students interviewed consider as research? How can it be linked with the creative process of designing?

As stated before, all interviewees expressed the opinion that design research was an integral part of high-quality design projects. When asked about their own projects, some had difficulties identifying what design research was and which aspects of their work could be seen as research led. Thus, when talking about their own projects, high quality could also be achieved, at least for some interviewees, without integrating design research.

> "I believe in my case it is not absolutely ... necessary, I believe. It would maybe be better, it would be good. But it is not mandatory that I now do research, well research is maybe the wrong word now. [...] Study, a study maybe. But research, I would not know, in my case, what could be considered research. I am not sure, should, should it be research, the practical bachelor thesis, in theory? Well, should it?" (student).

This quote demonstrates how unsure the student feels regarding the task: What does a practical bachelor's project entail, and does it have to involve design research in some way?

All interviewees agreed that the possibility to successfully integrate design research into a practical project hinged upon the nature of the said project. They stated that there was no general relationship between research and design, but this relationship had to be developed specifically for each project.

When asked directly what design research might be in the context of their projects, all students mentioned inquiring how their topic had been dealt with in design history. Additionally, students reported doing competitor analysis and examining what was being designed currently in their chosen field. Two students talked about experimenting with materials in a research-led process in order to find out how to best use a material for a given purpose. Lastly, reflecting on oneself was also considered research by one student.

> "Yes, well, there is also that ... doing research within yourself ... Which then simply is very hard to prove or, oh, I always find that to be so ... difficult ... because I cannot verify it with anything, I cannot quote anything. These are only my own perceptions in that case in part ... yes. And also such shapes develop certainly from a certain stock, which enters my head through my eyes, through a filter into my brain and then ... you cannot just go back to an origin like that" (student).

Two of the students interviewed clearly expressed disdain for having to reference other people for their practical bachelor's project. Specifically, they did not wish to look for sources on which to base the shapes and objects they created. "I also do not really like reading, maybe there is a connection with that. That I just think: Pf, now I sit down again and look through what other people have thought. I just simply prefer to generate myself rather than to adopt others" (student).

> "I want to do a distinct project, with my clear thoughts, being allowed to formulate them in such a clear way and I also do not find it to be necessary that a person has to refer to any and everything that people have already investigated and done before. Um, is of course good, is always more substantiated, is always, makes for a more complete picture. But I do not always find it necessary, not imperative" (student).

The other four students interviewed did not express negative attitudes towards having to incorporate research into their projects. One student who is very apt at linking research and practice stated that they had difficulties doing research in the same competent way as they designed or built prototypes. They simply did not possess the skills to do so. The more insecure students felt about scientific writing the harder it would be for them to integrate research into their practical bachelor's projects. The student who raised the issue attributed their difficulties to a lack of preparatory training. They wished for more support in scientific writing and research-based work during their bachelor's studies.

Research-oriented work was also seen as beneficial for designing. In the opinion of one student, field research helped them to explore how their topic and the intended object were embedded in everyday life. That enabled them to assess functionalities, find justifications for what they set out to do, and to tap into perspectives of the target group on how to potentially use the object. The students stated that research helped them align their designs with actual needs and ways of application. "In order for me not to design something that is only happening in my perspective, but that really from the entirety of the target group that I aim at so to say, that I consider them" (student).

> "Well it does influence how, that simply, that ideas can once again be overturned by research or just respectively can be revised. Research obviously also always reflects a lot and, I believe, often brings the designer, who sometimes maybe thinks of himself as artist, back to reality a little bit" (student).

Especially a commercial exploitation of design objects benefited from research in the view of the students. This might be due to the fact that to them design research primarily resembled user research.

One student found the formulating of a clear research question to be helpful because the question set a direction for their work which they could hold on to. With the research question they found it easier to decide which information, context, and sources had to be researched, what the scope of the question had to include, and what they could leave out. "And that first helped me, that I then had a clear research question very early on and then there again is anyway quite a big leeway" (student). In that way, they could focus on doing inquiries. "I simply set up my research in a way that I pick and choose specifically what, what I or what I believe will help me to further my design, yes" (student).

Thus, while the students pointed out the benefits of incorporating research-based working styles into design practice, they expressed great insecurities surrounding that task. Where did the difficulties stem from?

Ideas about design research, what it is and how it can be related to practice, differ among the course teachers. This fact was also addressed by the students. While some found it productive to be confronted with the different views and opinions of the teachers, others felt challenged by it. The differences in teachers' approaches centred around two questions: To what extent does knowledge have to be verbalised, and how and in what way should a research-based design process be structured?

During the consultations observed in the study, teachers told their students that they needed to be able to argue why they chose to design the project in the way that they did. A number of students felt challenged by that demand, and some even expressed a lack of understanding for this requirement. In one consultation, for example, a student presented different shapes that they liked for the design of their final object. The teacher asked how they arrived at the shapes. The teacher wanted to know why the student chose this or that design element and why they chose to solve a specific function in the given formal-aesthetic way. The student did not give answers to the questions posed but explained that the shapes had developed through their work and now felt harmonious. The teacher urged them to start thinking about the questions they had asked. A designer had to be able to account for the shapes they created. The student promised to think about these matters and closed the consultation by assuring the teacher that they had no unresolved questions at that point.

In an interview, the student explained that the task of analysing their design and classifying it according to design theory felt disruptive at the stage of work that they were in.

> "At the moment I find it hindering, because I have generated a shape out of my brain that I completely feel comfortable with [...] and now I intrinsically refuse to sit down with a book and look up whether the shapes are good for X [aim of the created artifact, substituted by authors for reasons of anonymity]" (student).
>
> "I understand the thought and I understand that one can build on what is already there and should in order to generate new knowledge, but ... it would, I just fear that this will lead me somewhere completely else, where I now no longer want to go, because I have to start constructing. Well these, one could do research forever, but at some point one has to know, that it is enough. Exactly. That is the difficulty at the moment" (student).

How are scientific-methodological ways of working able to support design processes and at which points do they come into conflict with creative-artistic practice? There is no easy answer to these questions based on the evaluation data at hand. Focusing one's topic and formulating a research question is a good example of the intricacies of the matter. One student, who was quoted above, was very happy about defining a clear research question early on in their project. They felt supported but not restricted by the focus offered through the means of a research question. Another student, on the other hand, felt bothered by the demand to specify their topic early on.

> "When I had to focus my topic, to find a research topic, I felt, um, held back. Well I noticed how long I had to grapple with it and that it rather worked to drive me crazy than to help me further my process. And at the end, after two weeks, I was without model or so. Because I approached this overly intellectual" (student).

Probably, the answer to the question of whether it is best to start a design project with a clear-cut topic and question rests on one's personal style and way of working (structured versus open, process-oriented). But it also depends on the approach to design and the notion of what design research is. Thus, the answers that the teachers in the courses gave to these questions also differed based on their personal styles and ideas of design / design research. A student had the following to say about her supervisors' positions:

"For example, focusing on the research question. One side says it is very important to have it and to work with it from the beginning on, the, the other side says, one, one can, the question can also pop up at the end. What is important, is to stay on the ball. I mean, staying on the ball is for both, both say to stay on the ball in any event" (student).

Based on the consultations observed, we can state that the different teachers supervising students exhibited different ideas about the relationship between creative-artistic practice and scientific-methodological approaches. This is represented by the fact that a more structured way of working was prescribed to the students by the project documentation template, while the instruction in the studio followed a more open, process-oriented approach. The students expressed appreciation for being given a structure to document their work. It served as an orientation but also made them feel safe, not having to start with a blank page when they wrote their report – which they mostly did at the very end of their final semester. Yet some students also reported that the structure offered by the research-oriented course felt overbearing or threatening at times, because it did not fit with their way of working or where they were at in their individual design processes. The scope of the students' design projects was so broad that a one-size-fits-all approach, both in the studio or in the research-oriented course, would always prove inadequate.

The multitude of teachers' perspectives found their way into student engagement with design and their practical bachelor's projects. It became clear that the students had been exposed to research-oriented courses and learned about the relevance of incorporating design research into high-quality design projects. The lack of ability to translate this general notion to their own projects may hinge upon a more formalistic view of working scientifically or doing research. This view then impacts negatively upon the work process. A research question, for instance, serves to help direct one's own attention, but it may change during the research process when necessary. Some students perceived the research question as an invariable value and felt restricted by its tight constraints, rather than adapting it according to their work process. Thus, it is important whether the students perceive the research question as a tool to help them structure their project or as constraint imposed on them. The need to document their work by using references offers a similar example. Some students felt that they had to quote 'each and every' author or designer working on the same topic, thereby missing the point that referencing fulfils specific tasks in an academic text and quotes are not to be given for the sake of quoting.

The results of the case study are consistent with the literature review presented in Part I on what hinders the establishment of a successful knowledge bridge: a shortage of time, a lack of competences in scientific writing or researching, as well as a vague understanding of the merits of incorporating research into design practice and about the aims of conducting research for a practical project.

Thus, teaching that wishes to support students in applying research to design practice needs to show students, in very specific ways, how elements of research may inform the design process. Students need time to practice scientific-methodological ways of working during their studies, for example, researching design history and applying it to the designs they have come up with. The teaching further needs to bear in mind that different types of student projects may merit different approaches to research.

Moreover, our research shows that notions of what is design research are contested among faculty – representing current discussions within the design discipline as to how design research may look, what methods are to be used, and how to create the relation between written language and design objects. While this may enrich intellectual discussion among students and teachers, the diversity of approaches can lead to confusion on the part of students. In the two courses that were evaluated, we found that teachers each focused on one working style – a more structured approach versus one more focused on the spontaneities of creative practice. In this way, students would benefit from a tighter linkage between the design studio and the research-oriented course, not having to make the connection themselves, but being supported by a closely intertwined course structure. We have seen that students who view the theoretical and practical bachelor's theses as one entity succeeded very well in combining research-related practices with their practical design process.

D4   Conclusion (phase 1)

Having analysed students' perspectives on applying research to design practice, we find that students have difficulties translating the general notion of design research which they hold to specific design projects. The reasons lie less in a general disdain for doing research, a sentiment that was found in older studies on design students' perspectives. Rather, the bachelor's students are overwhelmed by having to master the competences needed for doing research – such as academic writing or analysing their designs with reference to design history – while at the same time creating an object for their final thesis. Many of them are at a loss as to how to inspire the creative process by engaging with design research. This is largely due to a rather formalistic idea of how doing research can look.

Developing the ability to reflect on one's work by distancing oneself from one's own ideas and preferences seems a crucial capacity for successfully establishing a knowledge bridge between research and practice. In order to do so, students need time, but also experience in how to connect analytical-methodological styles of work with creative-artistic practices in different stages of a design process. ◄

E   Main competences in a design process (phase 2)

In order to work on making a change to academic design education, it is first essential to understand what kinds of problems students have when carrying out research in design. For this reason, an examination of the main competences needed in a holistic design process was chosen as an approach and a second case study with students of the sixth semester of the "Manual & Material Culture" BA programme was conducted.

The study mainly focused on finding out where students had difficulties in combining design research-related tasks with design practice. To this end, the study built upon the concept of competences developed in education and psychology (Schaper, 2012). Fink (2010) explained that there are only a few models for evaluating teaching in a competence-based way. The existing ones either fall into the category of performance tests or self-assessment tools for students on a very general level, not taking into account discipline-specific competence development (Braun et al., 2008; Paechter et al., 2007). Gelmez (2017) made an attempt to adapt these levels to design education but found that this approach still requires further research to develop models for measuring discipline-specific competences. Thus, the existing approaches could not be used for the aim set out by this study.

Moreover, there was no adequate existing taxonomy of competences in design that served the need of classifying all main competences needed for conducting a successful practice-led or practice-based research process; the competences first had to be deduced and defined. As a consequence, for the preparation of the case study, the human-centred design process model (Dittenberger, 2019) used for design teaching, which builds on Huber's (2013) concept of learning by research as well as Candy & Edmond's (2018) guideline for carrying out practice-led research in the creative arts, was used as a starting point. This design process is divided into the phases *Inspire, Collect*, with the sub-categories *Collect-Input, Collect-Output* and *Collect-Design, Design* and *Evaluate*. For the implementation of the study, the process phases were translated into six main competence areas: (1) project planning (Inspire), (2) design research (Collect-Input), (3) project conceptualisation (Collect-Output, Collect-Design), (4) designing (Design), (5) model building (Evaluate) and (6) final project presentation. All the process phases described in this process model were examined with regard to the main competences required for carrying out design research studies as well as for designing and prototype construction. Based on this, a questionnaire was developed that could be used by students to self-assess competences needed for practice-led as well as practice-based research. Starting from the human-centred design process, competences were identified in the six areas of planning a project, of doing design research, of conceptualising a project, of designing, of model building, and of presenting the project (see Table 4), and a questionnaire translating the competences for student self-assessment was created.

The questions within the Project Planning category, which corresponds to the Inspire process phase, encompass both competences in the self-organisation and time management of the design project, the ability to define a topic and a question to be examined therein, and the definition of the objective of the design project. Within the category of Design Research, which corresponds to the Collect-Input process phase, questions were raised about the ability to develop a study plan; the knowledge, selection, implementation, and analysis of different research methods; the ability to carry out a comparative analysis of design work and to carry out literature research and analysis on the topic; as well as the ability to adequately document the design research carried out. At the end of the questions in this category, the interviewees were asked to freely mention five known methods of design research. In accordance with the Collect-Output process phase, questions about the ability to point out problem areas within the independently selected topic area and to develop tasks were formulated in the Conception category. Based on this, questions regarding the ability of the project's initially formulated questions to be refined based on the knowledge gained and the addressees of the design project were drawn up. According to the Collect-Design process phase, further questions were asked within this category to enable a design brief to be created with regard to the technical-practical, aesthetic, and symbolic design function. Subsequently, the ability to develop a concept was assessed as well as maintaining the project focus during the work process, the flexibility required to adapt goals in the course of the project based on the knowledge gained and to carry out material research and development.

Corresponding to the Design process phase, the Design category asked about the ability to outline techniques, knowledge of craft-based and digital model construction, the integration of the addressees of the project into their own design process, and the ability to make a connection between design research and their artistic design process. At the end of the questions in this category, interviewees were asked to freely mention five design methods. For the Model Building category, questions were posed regarding the ability to discuss their design, the ability to cooperate interdisciplinarily, technical construction planning for building the prototype, and skills in terms of crafts-based and digital prototype construction. The Evaluate process phase was also assigned to the Implementation category and addressed questions

Project planning

- ► self-organization and time management
- ► definition of a topic
- ► definition of a preliminary research question
- ► definition of the project objectives

Design research

- ► development of a study plan
- ► knowledge and selection of research methods
- ► conduction of research on the project's context
- ► conduction of research with the target group of the project
- ► conduction of a comparative analysis of design work
- ► conduction of a comparative literature analysis
- ► documentation of complete research process

Conception

- ► identification of problem areas
- ► definition of work tasks
- ► refinement of research question
- ► final definition of the project's target group
- ► development of a design briefing
- ► overall design concept development
- ► upholding of the project focus throughout the development process
- ► material research and material development

Design + Model Building

- ► sketches
- ► involving the target group in the design process
- ► model building – craft based and digital
- ► linkage of research and design
- ► incorporation of feedback from tutorials
- ► prototype construction planning
- ► prototype construction – craft based and digital
- ► ability to cooperate with other experts
- ► involving the target group in the prototype construction
- ► ability to integrate the feedback of the target group

Presentation

- ► sketches
- ► visualizations – 2D and 3D
- ► presentation skills – staging, verbal and written

Table 4: Category chart of key-competencies in a design process

concerning the ability to integrate and incorporate feedback from the addressees of the design project into the design phase. As a final point regarding the questions concerning the main competences, the Presentation category asked about the ability to use one's own outlining technique, the mastery of 2D and 3D programmes, and the preparation of the project for presentation purposes. It also included an assessment of the students' verbal and written project presentation skills. The case study was carried out using a mixed-methods, quantitative and qualitative, study approach. The questionnaire created was used by students as a quantitative self-assessment tool, which was triangulated with a qualitative analysis of student perspectives on using a proposed process guide. The case study pursued the goal of answering the question: "Can the required main competences within each individual phase of a design process provide information about the problems in building bridges between design research and design practice?"

After the preparation of the questionnaire, students in their sixth semester received, building on the basics already practised in the previous semesters, specific theoretical input about the design process methodology and design research methods they could use to support their work in the first unit of the semester. Aside from lecture notes explaining the process methodology, they were also provided with a presentation that included works from past semesters, showing how students had integrated research and practice in different types of design projects. During this presentation, students were given information on the two types of research they could choose from, practice-led research/research with and for design or practice-based research/research through design, and how these types of research fit with the different types of design projects: applied research and experimental development. Furthermore, students received a process documentation InDesign template which they were to fill in so that by the end of the semester, they would not only present a final practical project, but have a written documentation (including literature reviews, research findings, design process, photos, etc.) of their project, which was to be assessed as well.

The study was carried out with students from the sixth semester because this final semester is an indicator of the extent to which the students understood the concept developed in the curriculum of the interrelating content of previous semesters. Since the "Manual & Material Culture" BA programme is a very young design study programme that addresses contemporary issues in design and production, specific self-evaluation is essential for the development of the programme.

Students were selected for interviews by the teachers on the basis of the type of final project they were working on in order to include students with a more straightforward product design project as well as students who were doing material research and experimental development projects.

For the quantitative part of the study, the questionnaires, all students of the sixth semester were involved and asked to fill in the provided forms anonymously. The evaluation of the questionnaire forms was conducted by an external social scientist. Concerning the qualitative part of the study, it was important that all students committed to the interviews on a voluntary basis and were happy to talk about their experiences. In order to ensure confidentiality and to protect students, who would be assessed by the teachers at the end of the semester, the interview files were kept by the external social scientist who conducted the interviews. Results from the interviews were only communicated to the teachers after the students had received their final grades for the study programme. Furthermore, interview results were anonymised by the social scientist, guaranteeing that no personal data was revealed through the communication of the study results.

The specific situation of the Covid-19 pandemic that transpired over the course of the semester in which the study was run led to several challenges. While theoretical inputs could be provided digitally and the interviews could be conducted and recorded via Zoom software without any major problems, the students were limited in terms of the practical implementation of their projects due to the temporary closure of the workshops of the university during lockdowns. However, this problem was successfully addressed by extending the semester from the end of June to the end of September 2020.

In a first trial of the tool developed, students were asked to fill out the questionnaire at the beginning of summer semester 2020 and at the end in order to assess how they viewed their competence development over the course of the semester. During the semester, students received tutorials after which they were asked to evaluate the gain of skills in each of the evaluation categories. Since self-assessment only goes so far in depicting competence development, the questionnaire developed was supplemented by an external assessment of student competences that was based on the same outline of competences used for creating the self-assessment tool. A second questionnaire was developed which teachers had to use to determine the degree to which each student possessed the competences in question at the end of the semester. This external assessment was then compared with the students' self-assessment. Using a mixed-methods approach, teachers were also asked to continuously document difficulties students experienced in the last semester while working on their final design project, relating specifically to competences that might be lacking in order to conduct a successful practice-led or practice-based research process – in a qualitative way. These results were then triangulated with the quantitative analysis of the questionnaires. Lastly, six problem-centred interviews with students were conducted at the end of the semester, aimed at determining how students view competence development as well as the teaching and teaching materials used in their final semester.

The following subchapters provide information on the results of the quantitative and qualitative methods of the mixed-methods study conducted as part of the project.

E1 Quantitative assessment of design students' main competences: Questionnaire

The questionnaires for students and teachers were structured in six categories (project planning, design research, project conceptualization, design, model building, and presentation) and comprised a total of 49 seven-point Likert scale questions as well as two open questions. In order to analyse the self-assessment data of the students at the beginning and at the end of the sixth semester, all scores given by each single student under each main competence area were summed up and the respective medians were computed to assess central trends of the distributions. As the medians relate to values lying at the midpoint of the frequency distributions of observed values, they show central trends of the number distributions.

	Formalized questions	Open questions	Maximum value possible
Projekt planning	6	–	12
Design research	12	1	84
Conceptualization	10	–	70
Designing	5	1	35
Model building	9	–	63
Presentation	7	–	49

Table 5: Overview of questions per category

Comparing student self-assessment and assessment by teachers, the differences in scoring were analysed. Because the scales at hand are ordinal, and in order to assume as little as possible about the underlying distributions, we employed a non-parametric test (Verma & Abdel-Salam, 2019). Given that there are three groups of assessments (self-assessment by students and external assessment by two teachers), a one-way ANOVA on ranks was chosen, for example, the Kruskal-Wallis test (Kruskal & Wallis, 2012), with the assumption being that the students score differently than the teachers do. In other words, the null hypothesis being that there is no difference in medians between these three groups of assessments.

In case the null hypothesis was rejected, pair-wise Mann-Whitney-U-tests (Weaver et al., 2017) were used to find the pair(s) of groups with different medians. Furthermore, the assessments done by the two teachers were compared by using the Wilcoxon signed-rank test (ibid.). The questionnaires were sent out to 19 students at the beginning and the end of the semester. Two teachers filled out questionnaires assessing each student at the end of the semester.

Semester 6

	Beginning	End
Projekt planning	17	19
Design research	17	16
Conceptualization	16	14
Designing	17	13
Model building	17	13
Presentation	16	13

Table 6: Overview of the completed questionnaires per category

The following paragraphs provide information on the results of the quantitative assessment.

Look at how the students self-assessed their competences in all the main competence categories at the beginning and the end of semester, quite low assessments were found. After normalising the scores, roughly 3.2 points were reported for each main category. The students assessed their main competences in all the categories at only about a third of that. The highest scores can be found for design research and project conceptualisation. These scores are even higher at the beginning of the semester compared to the end.

Project planning

Looking at the medians, we can see that the students' assessment of competence levels drops from the beginning (13) to the end (10) of the semester (maximum possible 42), except when asked about their ability to determine a question within their chosen topic. Big differences between the normalised scored at the beginning and the end of the semester can be found for the ability to structure and organise (about -1 point) and to develop a timetable (roughly 0.7 points). With the exception of the ability to structure and organise (-1), the medians are stable from the beginning to the end of the semester.

Design research

An examination of the medians reveals a rather low self-assessment of competences in design research, with all medians being lower than half of the maximum points possible. Design research as a competence area has received the highest scores compared to the other main competence categories. However, the median at the beginning of the semester (30) declines until the end (27) (maximum possible 84).

Project conceptualisation

The overall situation is comparable to the other main competence categories. All the medians are well below half of the maximum points possible and all the medians, again, drop over the course of the semester (23 to 17.5, maximum possible 70). Looking at the answers given by the students, the biggest declines in assessment of competence can be found for carrying out and documenting material research as well as material development. For both, there is an approx. -0.8 point drop. While for the first statement the median also drops (-1), the one for the second statement is stable. It might be the case that a few students with a lot of confidence lost a good portion of it, while the rest the group remained at their starting level.

Design

Overall, the medians are low compared to the maximum number of points that can be acquired (35), and they further decline over the course of the semester (from 9 to 8). The biggest drop is in the students' ability to use 3D programmes, -1 point. The second statement that is assessed quite differently at the end of the semester is the one regarding the ability to integrate potential users, where we find a decrease of 1.1 points.

Model building

Within this category, not a single student's statement saw a rise in medians. The median at the beginning of the semester dropped from 18 to 14 at the end of the semester (maximum possible 63). The biggest difference, about -1 point, between the assessments can be found for the design and implementation of the students' projects using a 3D programme as well as their ability to integrate future users of their project into their design process with the help of design research methods.

Drops in the amount of -0.5 points can be found for the assessment of the ability to do analog prototype construction and to create a plan for their prototype. The biggest shift in medians can be found for the ability to construct analog prototypes (-1) and to integrate future users into the design process (-1).

Presentation

Concerning this category, the medians remain below the half-way point of the maximum points possible (49), relating to the confidence in competence assessment for presentation skills. The median at the beginning of the semester dropped from 14 to 12 at the end of the semester.

Self-assessment vs external assessment

Our study shows that the teachers tended to give higher scores than the students themselves did. As a result of our statistical analysis, it can be stated that the differences in scoring are not significant. This is to say that although the teachers scored higher, the more points they gave were not spread evenly. When comparing the assessments by the two teachers, we find a significant difference regarding project planning. The assessments tended to differ in terms of the main competences of design, model building, and presentation. The explanatory nature of these results is limited by the fact that they rely upon a very small sample size. In order to assess whether there was a significant difference between the self-assessment and the external assessment, we employed the Kruskal-Wallis test, comparing the scores given by students at the end of the semester with the assessments given by the two teachers. Despite both teachers giving their students higher scores than the students' self-assessment, we only witnessed one significant difference with respect to two competence categories: design and presentation.

E2   Qualitative assessment of design students' main competences: Problem-centred interviews

In order to supplement the quantitative data assessing competence levels and development in the study programme, a qualitative approach was taken to identify student perspectives on working with the suggested process guide, the knowledge bridge between design research and design practice, and their view of their competence development over the semester. Six problem-centred interviews (Witzel, 2000) were conducted with the students. The results from these interviews were then triangulated with the quantitative analysis of the questionnaires. Due to the specific situation of the Covid-19 pandemic that transpired over the course of the semester in which the study was run, the interviews were conducted via Zoom and also recorded by this software. The audio files were used for transcription and analysis, with the interviews lasting from 35 to 55 minutes. Students were selected for interviews by the teachers on the basis of the type of final project they were working on. Furthermore, the transcripts were analysed by content analysis and the interview results were anonymised.

Students' perspectives on using the process guide

Students reported that the information on the design process and the two types of research they could choose from, practice-led research/research with and for design or practice-based research/research through design, at the beginning of the final semester was clear and easy to understand. Nevertheless, when they were asked how they perceive the use of the suggested process guide, the answers ranged from very positive views, with students finding its application useful for planning and structuring their design process, to students criticising it, saying that a design process should not lead to standardisation since designers may go about designing in various ways, for example, by focusing on the technical or using a more artistic approach. It was also suggested to compose different process guides for practice-led research and for practice-based research. In general, students found that it would have been helpful to be confronted with designing as a process a lot earlier in the study programme than was being done.

Knowledge bridge between design research and design practice

It seemed evident to all the students interviewed that the final practical project had to be accompanied by systematic documentation that embedded the project into design research, theory, and history. The reasons given for this need were the following: combining design practice and design research is a skill that graduates of a bachelor's programme need to master in order to participate in the current discourse on the discipline and to do professional design work; it helps when presenting one's work to potential employers; integrating design research helps designers be able to make arguments for what they have created; and as a result it enhances how the final object can be presented. Yet the students explained that it was challenging to holistically connect design research with their practical projects in their final semester. Some of them found it easier to do so when they were embarking on practice-based research (for example, material studies). Concerning practice-led research, they stated that the task of bringing together cultural background, reactions from subjects on their designs, design history, and a holistic reflection on the design process, which was expected when designing a product, was almost overbearing.

The results of the mixed-methods study, consisting of a quantitative survey by means of a questionnaire for self-assessment of the core competences in each phase of a design process and qualitative problem-centred interviews, provide an initial insight into the problem of building bridges between design research and design practice.

It is shown that the cohort studied actually scored their competencis quite low. The students assessed their main competences in all categories at only about a third of the points that could have been scored. The students rated their competencies lower at the end of the semester than they did at the beginning.

	Median at the beginning of the semester	Median at the end of the semester	Maximum value possible
Projekt planning	13	10	42
Design research	30	27	84
Conceptualization	23	17.5	70
Designing	9	8	35
Model building	18	14	63
Presentation	14	12	49

Table 7: Overview of the medians for each competence category

The results from the problem-centred interviews with students from the sixth semester, on the other hand, indicate that students did feel confident about their design-related abilities, being able to carry out a final project from beginning to end. Students mentioned that they wished they had been taught the applied design process earlier during the study programme, yet all but one felt positive about their skills to carry out all the necessary steps. Obviously, each student indicated specific areas they felt better equipped in and others where they identified potential for further development. Being able to focus their project during the project planning stage, hand-drawing skills in the design stage, as well as the ability to connect research with practice are amongst the least developed skills among the students, in their opinion.

Regarding the suggested process guide, the interviewees differed in their views. While some found it very easily applicable to their work process and stressed how it helped them structure their project, some did not seem to know about its content or criticised that they felt constrained working with it. It was emphasised that the process guides should be introduced earlier during the study programme and should also be reduced in size to make them more accessible. The necessity of doing design research and integrating it into their final projects was unchallenged by all interviewees. Some exhibited a quite vague notion of what design research is, yet again, they all wished they would have been introduced to design theory and history more and at earlier stages of their studies. Building a true knowledge bridge between design research and practice in their final projects was seen as a challenging endeavour, due to the holistic nature of the design process. Yet an endeavour that was worthwhile when one considered the quality of the projects and the graduates' chances of establishing themselves in a professional environment as independent designers or employees.

E3   Conclusion (phase 2)

What did we learn from our attempt to understand the difficulties of integrating design research into design practice with the help of an analysis of the main competences in each phase of a design process? In conclusion, it can be stated that an understanding of the necessity of a productive connection between research and practice, which underlies the discipline of design, must be developed at the very beginning of design education from the BA level on and become a self-evident design culture during the course of studies. Furthermore, it can be concluded that the application of and reflection on structured design processes must be taught and practised from the beginning of the course of study on the basis of a terminology commonly used by all design teachers. The theory and practice of design processes and a generally valid language convention for design can thus be internalised by the end of the bachelor's programme.   Through the continuous application of a subject-specific design and research culture from the first semester onwards, the self-assessment of prospective designers about their own competences should be improved and the self-confidence essential for creative workers in inter-disciplinary projects strengthened.

The surprisingly poor values in the self-assessment of the students studied suggest that design teaching has to react to this issue. With regard to the complex requirements that designers face after a BA degree, the concept of design teaching has to evolve in order to synthesise the core competences required in both areas. The conclusion is drawn that the goal of contemporary design teaching on the BA level should be to impart a generalist, methodologically robust but open and solution-oriented approach to linking research and practice, which both addresses the multidimensionality of the demands on the discipline of design itself and imparts the scientific methodological competence to deal with them productively and self-confidently.

Concerning the students' feedback on the process guide, the use of the process guidelines has proven to be helpful for explaining the desired bridge between research and practice to students as they mentioned the need for its integration from the very beginning of all specialisations within the bachelor's programme. In addition to these concrete and proven process guidelines, for practice-led research or applied research and practice-based research or experimental development, it is necessary to establish an unambiguously communicable, methodologically robust but open process in the sense of experimental research, which can be adapted to the needs of individual design approaches. The question of how academic research can be conducted within individual creative practice has been discussed intensively in the past decades in academia. Mäkelä and Nimkulrat (2018) presented the approach of using documentation as a support tool for the reflection process on practical design work. Nonetheless, further research work is necessary in order to draft a holistic process proposal in the field of artistic-scientific research that does justice to the different requirements of the design disciplines and the academic standards. ◄

F   Experiments (phase 3)

The third stage of the RIDE project focused on the role of design research and the linking of design research and practice within designers' work. A qualitative study, "Design-Scientific Research: Investigation of a Process Methodology", was conducted, linking experiments with observations, interviews, as well as reflective discussions. The study aimed to counter a perceived lack of definition and process guidelines in this research area to generate hypotheses to set up a new guideline for it. The study followed an experimental approach, enabling eight students from the "Manual & Material Culture" bachelor's programme to contribute to projects with professionals. As observing participants as well as participating observers, they were able to gain insights into research, work, and reflection processes (for example, Diekmann, 2007; Fromm, 2012). The students' experiences and observations were documented within a digital research diary guided by the accompanying questionnaires including questions ranging from current work steps to aesthetic and design-led decision processes to personal learnings. They also conducted two qualitative guided interviews with the professionals, which were recorded and logged.

   Within the study, two experiments were carried out to provide information on the following questions:
   ► How and in what form do designers research the context of
     their project?
   ► Which knowledge / know-how do the designers draw on in their work?
   ► Is design research taking place? If so, in what form?
   ► How do design research and design practice combine in the
     execution of the task?
   ► How do designers describe their work processes?
   ► Do the designers reflect on or contextualise the works they create?
     If so, how?

The results of the experiments should enable the following central questions to be addressed:
   ► How can the creative, design, and craftsmanship processes be
     described systematically?
   ► What form of research is carried out in design practice to acquire
     basic knowledge of the project task?
   ► Can research components be identified in "normal" practical projects?
     If so, which ones?

- ► How and in what form can knowledge be derived from practical action in order to make a contribution to extending or deepening general knowledge in an area?
- ► What methods can be used to meet the scientific requirement of contextualising the resulting work?
- ► How can a process manual for the field of design-scientific research or artistic-scientific research be created from the insights gained?
- ► What innovative and practice-oriented teaching formats can be developed to strengthen the educational development in tertiary design education and beyond?

F1   Experiment I - Patchwork kitchen (handgedacht)

Handgedacht is a Viennese six-member design studio and carpentry specialised in the design, planning, and production of custom furnitures, living rooms, offices, retail outlets, and exhibitions. In their work, they attach particular importance to focusing on their customers' wishes and cooperating with them.

The design concept of the patchwork kitchen originated from a collaboration with students in 2016, which needed a kitchen for their shared flat but did not have the necessary budget that the mostly well-earning customers of carpentry work do. This led to the idea of using resources cost-effectively (money, material, and labour), in which customers were actively involved by, for example, researching which kitchens were already on the market, reusing certain parts, and/or actively involving customers in the production process.

Figure 4: Outcome experiment 1 (Photo: Korab)

Figure 4: Construction work for the experiment,
Cocreation and manufacturing process (Photo: NDU)

For handgedacht, the experimental approach is intended to achieve three aims. First, the desire to actively cooperate with customers, to give them the opportunity to participate in a more cost-effective development of a furniture / interior design and not to be forced due to tight budgets to purchase this from discounters. Secondly, they want to ensure that the production is as sustainable as possible, which leads to considerations regarding the use of existing resources, recyclability, and repair. Thirdly, they think that production is not a straightforward, but rather a participatory process that allows for creativity and the emergence of new ideas.

It is precisely the fact that the individual steps in production processes are often already predetermined that inspired handgedacht to develop their approach and to incorporate applied research to some extent. On the basis of their experiences, they want to intuitively design, freeing themselves as much as possible from constraints and creating space for experimentation. In this way, industry is not regarded as an outside entity, but rather as a part of the whole. The team is aware of what the industry can do, experimenting with it and using its resources (for example, the use of the possibilities of Industry 4.0 in the context of the production of a carpentry workshop).

Figure 5: Outcome experiment 1 (Photo: Korab)

Figure 6: Installation for the Ceramic Museum Scheibbs (Photo: Schranz)

F2   Experiment II - Brown tulips (Kristin Weißenberger)

Kristin Weißenberger is a Viennese ceramist and visual artist who wishes to explore the relation of natural processes and materials with man-made objects by frequently using ceramics in combination with biological material.

"Brown tulips" were objects for a five-piece display case wall made of porcelain, silicone, and sculptural elements in process interaction with form and material for the group exhibition "Loam-RE: Tonindustrie Scheibbs", which took place in Scheibbs' Ceramic Museum from June to October 2021. The exhibition project dealt with the history of the sound industry in Scheibbs, Lower Austria, and the ceramics museum exhibited the collection. The aim was to react and respond to the past presented from one's own current artistic position.

Initially, the project was characterised by feminist reflections on the engagement with the historical artists of the sound industry. Within the project development, however, questions of representation had arisen regarding the concept of "nature". Starting from the abstract aestheticisation of nature in Expressionism and, at the same time, the beginning of new forms of industrial organisation in the 1920s, modes of representation and views of nature became a topic. Thus, the impacts of what is known today as the Anthropocene were addressed. Through the process-based development, questions about the effectiveness or agency of material were also investigated.

The individual implementation steps of "Brown tulips" were more practice-led than planned. Looking back, they can be defined as 1) finding an approximate conceptual approach with working title, 2) material and shape search, 3) experimental phase, producing samples, investigation of different aesthetics, 4) evaluation and evaluation, 5) refining the conceptual approach/ writing, 6) generation of real objects on this basis, 7) planning of the installation setup in the 3D programme, 8) construction of displays and scenography, as well as 9) construction on site.

The students' perspective which emerged within the reflective discussions with the RIDE project team could lead at first glance to the assumption that design research and practice rather take place side by side, but a deeper analysis of the description of the working processes within the surveys as well as of the expert interviews with the company's heads shows that creative, design, and craftsmanship processes are indeed strongly intertwined. It has to be considered here that the students were perhaps not fully aware of that because the context of the project they were involved in was not made explicit from the beginning and they learned more about the idea behind the concept as well as of the knowledge and experience behind the company's working processes at later stages of the experiment and especially through the expert interviews.

Any reform of design education has to start by raising the design students' awareness of the necessary intertwining of design research and practice. However, students can greatly benefit from being involved in such experiments. This study showed that design students can gain broad knowledge by engagin in practice or doing experimental projects. The interaction and collaboration with professionals illustrated the relevance of familiarising design students with spaces, target groups or potential viewers, materials, and techniques, as well as of interacting with materials. Besides that, the students experienced the benefits of linking design research and practice as well as of exchanging and collaborating with others for the expansion of perspectives, knowledge, and skills.

Figure 7: Working process (Photo: NDU)

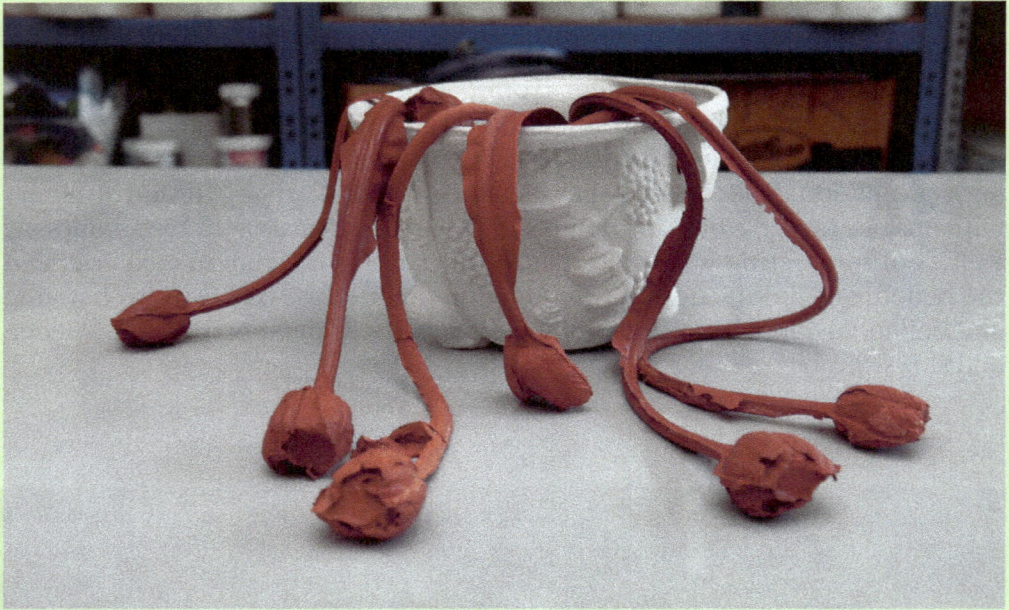

Figure 8: Working process (Photo: NDU)

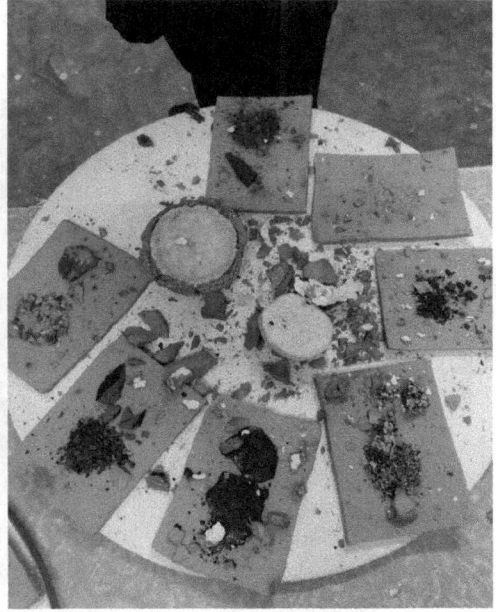

Figure 9: Working process (Photo: NDU)

Considering these results, the quality of design teaching could profit from a guideline or curriculum which gives students more space and time for practice-oriented, experimental work.

The students' statements on the surveys as well as the reflective discussions with the RIDE project team lead to the assumption that they could take a lot from the experiment for their future professional activities. "Experiment II" illustrated how the linking of empirical and practical knowledge as well as experimenting with materials and techniques can generate new knowledge.

Moreover, the project revealed the relevance of reflection and discussion processes to gain an external view. The regular expansion of one's perspective as well as scrutinizing familiar work routines and methods help to develop one's own professional skills continuously. Therefore, the experts benefited from the students' participation in the project as well.

From our perspective, "Experiment II" showed that it would be necessary to not only define cultural-scientific, theoretical research as design research but also experiments, which are a form of practice-based research.

93   Experiments

Figure 10: Working process (Photo: NDU)

F3 Learnings from the experiments in the RIDE project

Overall, it can be said that designers need to acquire sound theoretical and practical knowledge and skills about the world around them, potential target groups, trends, materials and technologies, social and economic issues, as well as about design and aesthetics per se. They never stop learning and grow professionally through their experiences, actively interacting with materials and experimenting, through succeeding as well as apparently failing which can lead to the development of new ideas and concepts. Students have to expand their awareness of the need for these processes as well as for the continuously intertwining of design research and practice. They benefit greatly from being actively involved in real projects of design and craft enterprises during their studies, which allow them to learn more about the practical implementation of knowledge, skills, professional experiences, and ideas in the realisation of concepts Besides that, they should also be encouraged to leave their comfort zones of familiar materials, techniques, and routines by working in a more practice-oriented way as well as gaining new knowledge and skills by implementing research in design practice.

94

While "Experiment I" was more structured and planned beforehand and dealt with concrete objects of use, "Experiment II" was more artistically oriented, specifically to the focus of the exhibition as well as the expert's ideas.

The aim of the first experiment was not to develop a new concept, but to analyse an already existing concept within the framework of the study, which partly led to work routines which had already been tried out. Apparently, there were hardly any reflection and discussion processes between the experts and students, apart from the exchange as part of the interviews. The participants of "Experiment I" were more closely involved in practical tasks than the participants of "Experiment II", but mainly in the form of receiving work orders. In the second experiment, the students were more involved in brainstorming processes. The observing participants took over auxiliary tasks in earlier project stages, while the focus was on the reflection on and discussion of work processes later on.

In "Experiment I", the context of the project was not made explicit from the beginning and only became clear in later phases and as part of the expert interviews. By contrast, "Experiment II" started by discussing the background of the project and clarifying the idea behind the exhibition.

Both experiments illustrated the relevance of familiarising students with spaces, target groups or potential customers/viewers, materials, and techniques, as well as of interacting with material. Besides that, all experts the interviewed emphasised the need to regularly expand one's perspective, knowledge, and skills by linking design research and practice as well as exchanging with others.

Coming back to the initial research questions posed in this paper, the following paragraphs summarise the findings.How can the creative, design, and craftsmanship processes be described systematically?

Both artistic, craft, and product design projects are goal oriented. Without a specific objective (for example, a product, an exhibition, or astudy), planning the design process and developing a guideline for orientation is not possible. Thus, a clear objective must be defined at the beginning of each project. Depending on the project's context and background, a stronger or weaker focus on factors such as customers, exhibition, or event themes is necessary.

However, it is crucial to familiarise students with spaces (for example, buildings and showrooms) and target groups or potential viewers as well as to consider the human perception of form, colour, material, and surface. Besides that, designers have to carry out research on context, materials, and techniques and strive to broaden their knowledge and skills if they are helpful or necessary for their work. Within project processes, it can be highly beneficial to link empirical and practical knowledge by interacting with materials and testing different techniques. The project stages should be accompanied and documented by regular journaling and sketching.

An experimental approach paves the way for the generation of new knowledge and skills, as the development, adaption, and abandonment of ideas if they turn out to not be feasible lead to fresh ideas.

It has been shown that the design process steps carried out in the two experiments do not fundamentally differ from the well-known ones. As already explained above, the students were mainly involved in the implementation phase of the projects. Only in Experiment II were they also involved in the idea development phase.

What form of research is carried out in design practice to acquire basic knowledge of the project task? Can research components be identified in "normal" practical projects? If so, which ones?

No actual answer could be found to this question within the experiments, since, as mentioned above, the students were mainly involved in the implementation phase. Nevertheless, after the experiments, each of the professionals was asked about the steps concerning how the research was integrated into the "Patchwork kitchen" and "Brown tulips" projects.

Research was not understood and carried out in a strictly scientific sense. The research process was also not carried out solely for a project but acquired knowledge was to a large extent experiential knowledge that was developed over time. Regarding the implementation, there were no requirements given regarding the research process, study design, or choice of method. A comparative literature analysis of the project contexts was not carried out in the usual sense. Information from the media and possibly literature was collected based on one's subjective perception. The observation of the target groups of the projects was also not carried out by using social scientific methods, but rather as free observation or personal reflection by the professionals or the project leaders of "Patchwork kitchen" and "Brown tulips". However, experimenting with materials and manufacturing processes as well as journaling and sketching were certainly practised.

How and in what form can knowledge be derived from practical action, in order to make a contribution to extending or deepening general knowledge in an area?

The observation of the experiments showed that the projects examined did not provide evidence that general knowledge can be created through practical action. This may be due to the fact that this either does not happen in principle or that the practice-based, individual, and implicit methods of documentation and reflection are not suitable for synthesising general knowledge from practice, making it communicable, discussable, and connectable to scientific discourse.

What methods can be used to meet the scientific requirement of contextualising the resulting work? As already mentioned above, dealing specifically with the literature in order to analyse the project context or make a comparison with the project history was not a common practice in the practical design projects.

How can a process manual for the field of design-scientific research or artistic-scientific research be created from the insights gained? On this point, the study made it clear that a discussion of recognised research standards is indispensable in order to be able to propose a new process model.

What innovative and practice-oriented teaching formats can be developed to strengthen the educational development in tertiary design education and beyond? One finding of the study is that university students need to be made aware of existing and recognised research standards and trained in their implementation. This circumstance will be carefully addressed in the next project steps regarding the development of new teaching formats.

F4   Conclusion (phase 3)

The study was undertaken with the main goal of investigating ways of generating knowledge through practical design action and, where appropriate, documenting the individual process steps involved.

One of the questions of this study aimed at finding an answer to the question of how and in what form knowledge can be derived from practical action in order to make a contribution to extending or deepening the existing knowledge. The experiments conducted revealed that it could not be proven that new knowledge is generated through practical action. Rather, the results of the study suggest that scientific research does not equate to practical action, as all the necessary conditions to meet scientific research standards are lacking. For example, the results show that, in terms of the project approach, there was no comparative reivew of the literature or practical project work to prove that the project topic had not been researched before. The two project partners for the experiments stated that they had done research on their projects, but they also admitted that they were not doing so according to scientific standards. Furthermore, it became clear that within the project work, no clear and appropriate research question had been defined, and no research process, study design, and methods had been defined according to scientifically recognised working methods. Methods of analysis and reflection were also not identified. Although the project partners claimed to be conducting research, it must be noted that there is a clear difference to recognised scientific standards.

The working processes observed in the experiments conducted as part of the project indicate instead the possibility of research through experimental development. However, this research process would also require a completely different project setup, which was not found in the experiments conducted. Furthermore, this study was also unable to answer the question as to which methods were applied to contextualise the projects created.

The findings of the study thus reveal rather sobering insights with regard to the question of whether and how new knowledge is generated through practical design action. However, these findings still need to be differentiated with regard to the topic of research in design practice.

Conclusion 1: Is research relevant for practicing designers?

The study reveals how designers act in everyday life. They themselves do not talk about the fact that they are doing specific research. This may be due to the fact that it has no relevance for them in their everyday work, or that they have no prior knowledge about research in design according to scientific standards. The scientific standards referred to here originate from the *Frascati Manual* (OECD, 2015), which states that research activities should meet the five core criteria of being "novel, creative, uncertain, systematic, transferable and/or reproducible" (ibid., p. 45). Nevertheless, they mention methods such as exploration, material and process experimentation as part of their working practice.

Conclusion 2: Clarify understanding of terms

The findings of the study also indicate that there may be different understandings of research in practical design action. On the one hand, this is not surprising since there is also no unified definition of research in design to be found in the literature, and, on the other hand, the way in which research in design is handled varies. Designers who conduct research according to scientific standards do not call it that themselves, and designers who merely conduct explorations in their projects call this research work. This question is also unresolved in the university teaching and research context.

This grey area makes further development of the subject area itself difficult. For this reason, it is concluded that it will take the courage to engage with existing definitions of terms and ways of working in science, for example, as described in the *Frascati Manual*, and to develop the field of scientific design research.

Conclusion 3: Learning by observation

Even though the study was not able to generate any direct results for the set goals, the conclusion remains that the scientific method of observation could be further developed for designers. Observation of work processes of practical design action has the potential to uncover innovative working practices during creative production as well as make the applied actions more communicable and repeatable for practice.

For the following project steps, this circumstance will be further researched in order to be able to provide details within the guideline. Nevertheless, other methods could also be considered such as the compositional interpretation (Muratovski, 2016), for the material analysis of image, ornament, and form; or the Offenbach approach (Steffen, 2000), for the analysis of the formal aesthetic, technical, and symboli product function; or the visual spatial analysis (Bohnsack, 2006), for the analysis of the spatial project context.

A reform of design education for designers should take experimental work processes more into account. Students could benefit a lot from leaving their comfort zones of predefined tasks and prototypes as well as learning by doing. Openness to results encourages freely working and experimenting, testing out of different techniques, developing new ideas, and finding new solutions. However, in order to be able to use experimentation productively as a research practice, a formalised and scientifically usable method for documenting, communicating, and reflecting on the process and the results must accompany the experimental work. ◄

Teaching Research in Design

G   Process guidelines

Where do the results of our research project lead us with regard to the actual integration of research in design teaching?

In Part II of the publication, we described the research process of our RIDE project, which was conducted in four successive phases. Referring to our findings on the students' self-evaluation of their skills concerning conducting research in a design project as well as the practice of exploration of design practitioners in their design projects, it seems obvious to us that in order to guide students through a complex design process, design educators need to offer clear and structured guidelines for a holistic design process on the BA level that combines research and design practice, which students can use as the underlying basis for their work. This circumstance can in itself be seen as a paradigm shift in design studio culture, as teaching in this central course of a design education thus needs design teachers who combine both design research skills according to scientific standards and design practical knowledge in order to make this kind of teaching possible. Nevertheless, as mentioned in the Introduction to this publication, we are not attempting to scientify design in itself. Rather, the publication attempts to show product design students and design educators ways in which research can become part of their everyday design work. The difficulties and challenges of decades of different definitions of design research and their interpretations were highlighted with regard to the recognition of traditional scientific fields for knowledge generated through practice-based design research.

Even if the integration of research in design is now considered a prerequisite at the university level, it is still important for us to emphasise that not every design action necessarily has to include a research component. Muratovski (2016) stated that:

> "[d]esign endeavours can be pursued either for oneself (design as an inward-looking practice) or for the benefit of others (design as an externally-driven process). [...] When approached in an external manner [...] design can be seen as a problem-solving process that [...] is driven by research rather than style" (ibid., p. XXX).

Our attempt to present a holistic design process, which aims to combine both research and practical design components and builds the foundation of this publication, is based on Muratovski's reference to design for the benefit of others or as a problem-solving process. To be able to solve a problem, one has to understand it, ask why it has come to this, and develop approaches to work on solutions in a structured and comprehensible way. The work on solutions can therefore relate to the subject-object relationship, the context of use, a processing procedure, or the development of a new material.

Thus, the third part of this publication will be devoted to the attempt to define process guidelines on how research can be integrated into product design teaching. The stages of the research project described above enabled us to reflect on our own positions and to develop our own approaches according to the aims of the publication.

The comparison of the different positions on how research in design is defined and what is considered research in design makes it clear that there still seems to be a long way to go towards consolidating the positions. The professional field of designers is diverse, from the traditional orientation of industrial and product design to artistic design, to the extended areas such as service design, strategic design, or interaction design. The diversity of the professional fields that fall under the heading of design is also reflected by the directions in which research is to be conducted.

The review of the literature presented in chapter B has provided us with decisive insights. Research, whether conducted as basic research, applied research, or experimental development, follows standards that render the uniqueness of the research approach, the choice of methodology and methods, the conduct and documentation of the research work, and the conclusions drawn from it comprehensible and reproducible. Our examination of the "learning by research" approach, with the request that students actively engage in conducting research, from asking questions to choosing methods and reflecting on the results achieved with reference to the research question posed, has proved helpful and also confirmed the need for a concrete implementation guide. The study of the field of "artistic-scientific research" has shown a clear dividing line to our field of product design. This circumstance was particularly interesting to us because at the beginning of the research project, we originally thought we were looking for an artistic-scientific way of working in the context of research in design teaching. This aspect has therefore not been pursued further in this publication.

In addition, a comparison of the forms and definitions of design research has enabled us to narrow down and focus on the areas of "practice-based" and "practice-led research" for undergraduate students. For the development of the process guidelines, we took into account both the call for standards for practice-based research approaches and the evidence presented in the *Frascati Manual*, which points to the fact that higher education institutions need to decide which research approaches would be most appropriate depending on the field being taught. As the focus of this publication is on the profession of product design, the development of the process guidelines is led by the orientation on "research through design"; "practice-based research", or in other words, "applied research"; and on "research with and for design" as well as "practice-led research", or in other words, "experimental development". As also described in chapter B, we have excluded the area of basic research because of the focus on integrating research into design teaching at the BA level. In our view, it would overwhelm students at this point; therefore, we conclude that the introduction of this area of research is better suited to the MA level.

In the following, process guidelines for projects in the areas of applied research, on the one hand, and experimental development, on the other, are presented. It is important to emphasise that we view the guidelines as a support and a means of orientation within a complex design process and not as a strict regulation that allows no room for creativity. On the contrary, research work is a highly creative activity, and there is no standardised magic formula for the conduction of research methods in design. The approach to investigating a problem area requires a high degree of empathy, openness, and flexibility on the part of the researcher with regard to the choice of methods and the design of methodologies for carrying out the research methods. In our view, then, research is part of a holistic development process that should be consistent with the creative practices of design. The following proposed processes are illustrated by student projects from the "Manual & Material Culture" study programme. As already explained in chapter B.4, the field of applied research is based on the scientific standards of the social sciences discipline and the field of experimental development is based on the standards of the engineering and natural sciences disciplines. Furthermore, we will give a detailed description of an orientation period for students to start with planning their projects as well as how to structure student reflection on and evaluation of their projects.

G1   Project planning: Orientation

At the beginning of the chapter, we outlined the focus of our process guidelines in the directions of applied research and experimental development.

In particular, the analysis of the design teaching in the "Manual & Material Culture" course in the context of the "Research in Design Education" study has shown that especially on the BA level, the identification of topics, the definition of specific objectives, the positioning of the project with regard to the respective research aspect (applied / experimental), and the planning and structuring of the diploma project is a major obstacle for many students.

This insight brings us back to the main competences presented in chapter E and provides an opportunity to reflect again on what stage of the design process we want students to think about research in their design projects. In our study on the main competences, we divided a holistic design process into six phases. With reference to the results obtained so far, it can be concluded that addressing and actively integrating research must already take place at the project planning phase, for example, the self-organisation and time management of the project, the ability to define a topic and a question to be examined therein, and the definition of the objective of the design project.

In order to offer students the possibility to get an idea of what problem field and question they would like to address in their project before the beginning of the actual diploma semester, we plan to hold a two-day diploma workshop in the semester before. Based on our teaching experiences over the last few years, we have concluded that students are overwhelmed by working through all phases of the proposed process paths within the diploma semester. The aim of this preparation is therefore to focus the work in the sixth semester on either user studies and the design of the product or on material research and the design of a use case for the developed material.

Again, for both process paths, we encourage students to devote the fifth semester to basic research for their upcoming practical theses as part of their theoretical BA thesis. In the following, we will present the steps we propose that comprise a project preparation for either an applied research or experimental development project.

RESEARCH – Project Preperation
- ▼ selection of project area
- ▼ preliminary problem definition
- ▼ preliminary definition of research question
- ▼ comparative literature analysis
  (for example chronological examination, historical research, thematic analysis, methodological comparison, theoretical comparison, meta-analysis)
- ▼ comparative analysis of creative works within the selected area with regard to the technical, aesthetic and symbolic design function

Table 8: Phases of diploma project preparation

Since the research for the preparation of their theoretical BA thesis focuses on both the identification of a relevant problem and a research question as well as the comparative literature analysis of their chosen topic, we plan for the two-day diploma workshop to then concentrate on the preparation of a comparative work analysis. In doing so, comparable relevant product design examples or materials will be identified and comparatively analysed according to the technical, practical, aesthetic, and symbolic design functions according to the Offenbach approach (Steffen, 2000).

106

In the following subchapters, we will explain in more detail the two process guides that we have developed. In order to illustrate our approach, two final projects from the "Manual & Material Culture" study programme, which can be classified either as applied research or experimental development, are presented using excerpts from the project documentation developed in the Research Lab course and photographs of the prototypes created in the design studio course.

G2   Applied research

In order to be able to successfully design products, rooms, services, information, interactions, or new technical systems for people, it is essential for future designers to first of all put people at the centre of their design activities.

Human-centered product development is carried out at the intersection between social scientific research methods and the implementation of the research findings in the subsequent design process. For this reason, the human-centered design approach is chosen for the area of applied research or practice-led research and research with and for design.

As already described, applied research aims to generate new knowledge for a practical application. For the creation of human-centered design, it is necessary to understand both the people of the target group and the context of the product use as well as to develop and evaluate design proposals with people of the target group. That is why the mixed-methods approach from qualitative research and applied research is suggested for the research process for applied research in design.

Building on the revised Human-Centered Design ISO Standard 9241: 210 on product design aspects (Dittenberger, 2018), which was revised again in 2019 for use in design teaching (Dittenberger, 2019), the qualitative research process is used to study the wishes, needs, and the life context of the people of the target group. The qualitative research process is based on the understanding of research in the humanities and cultural sciences and regards the subject as the constructor of its reality. Results are put into practice during the research process and hypotheses and theories are generated. Flick (2009) described the research process as non-standardised qualitative research through the steps of selecting a research problem, systematic literature analysis, formulating the question, developing a project plan, selecting suitable methods, entering the field of investigation, data collection (documentation of the data and data analysis), and discussion of the results (ibid., p. 76).

This design process currently used in this area is divided into the phases of Inspire and Collect, with the subcategories of Collect-Input, Collect-Output, Collect-Design, Design, and Evaluate.

107

COLLECT - INPUT
► collection of user requirements
  (social science & design research methods)
► collection of technical
  and economic requirements
► collection of ecological requirements
► formulation of research question

INSPIRE
► ethnographic observations
► problem definition
► literature reviews

COLLECT - OUTPUT
► list of overall user requirements
► list of technical, ecological and
  economic requirements

Human-centered design process

COLLECT-DESIGN
► design briefing – overall user needs
► design briefing – practical, aesthetic
  & symbolic product functions
► creation of Personas

EVALUATE
► design prototype development
► user evaluation of the design
  – utility safety & comfort

DESIGN
► creation of use-cases
  creation of scenarios
  creation of storyboards
► design concept development
  (practical, aesthetic & symbolic product functions)
► co-design workshops
► design studies, model making

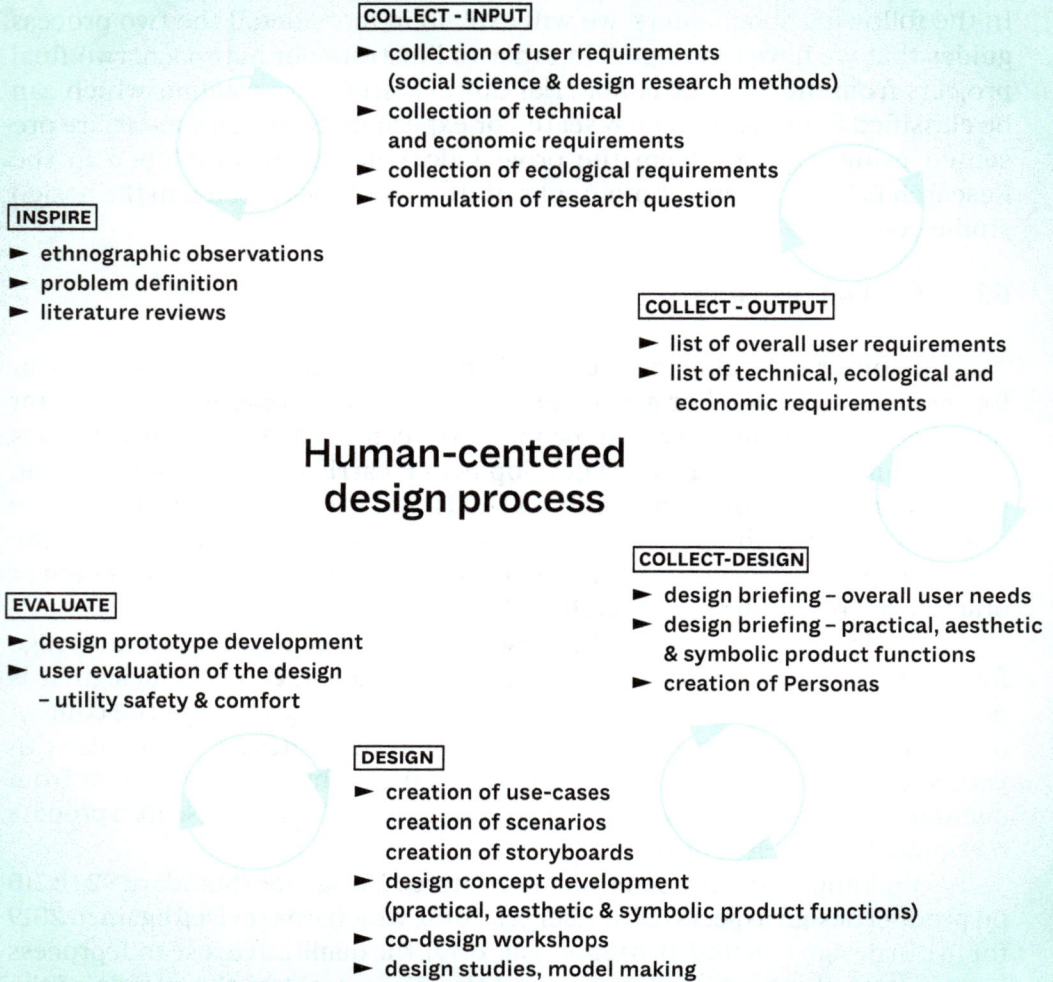

Figure 11: Human-centred design process (Dittenberger, 2019)

The focus in the Inspire process step lies on learning about the project's context. Methods of qualitative social research, such as observational and survey methods, are applied. Based on the results of these studies, problem areas within the project context can be identified and subsequently comparatively researched in the literature. In order to investigate the identified problem areas in more depth, further methods of qualitative social and design research are used in the Collect phase, such as interviews, focus groups, or cultural probes. After each method has been carried out, the aim is to focus the project on a specific problem as well as target group and to collect for this the human, technical, aesthetic, symbolic, ecological, and economic requirements. After the broad preparation of the requirements for the selected problem area, the results are evaluated, and a specific aspect is selected. For its processing, a research question and a design briefing for the project's practical, aesthetic, and symbolic functions (Schneider, 2005) is drafted which should be addressed in the following design phase. Furthermore, archetypal users – personas – are defined to ensure that the project focuses on the selected target group. The Design process phase is devoted to the development of design approaches, the conduction of design studies, and the building of analog/digital models. This process step also includes the active involvement and creative incorporation of feedback from the target group in the design development. The Evaluate phase represents the final step of the process. Before the final prototype is built, the project is finally evaluated by people of the target group to see whether the defined design briefing meets the requirements. In an iterative approach, the process is repeated until the evaluation results fulfil the defined requirements.

According to Muratovski (2016), there are different ways to conduct qualitative research, such as case studies, ethnographic research, phenomenology, historical research, or grounded theory. The research question serves as an indicator of which approach is most suitable for the project.

A case study is suitable for studying a complex phenomenon, such as a situation, an event, or a specific fact. To study a case, contextual information about the environment and the historical, economic, cultural, and social factors is collected. In order to maintain the focus of a case study, it is helpful to set parameters such as time and place, time and activity, or definition and context. Relevant data is collected via archival records or documents (for example, letters, reports, and articles).

Ethnographic research is used to study the people in the project's target group in detail, with a focus on their social interactions, behaviours, beliefs, and perceptions, as well as their environment. Data is collected through observation, participation in everyday life, cultural probes, or interviews.

The phenomenology study design is suitable for examining the views, social realities, and experiences of the people in the target group in more detail. The difference to the ethnography study design is that individuals are examined here instead of groups. Data is also collected here through observation, focus groups, and in-depth interviews.

Historical research is mainly used in design to conduct design history or trend research. Under the premise of not focusing on what and when but rather on why, data is collected through archive material, books, or documentation.

Grounded theory starts not from a theoretical approach as usual but aims at developing one from the data collected. Since this study design requires experience and interdisciplinary knowledge, this approach is mainly used from the PhD level on (ibid., 2016, pp. 48-104).

Since in the context of product and object design the focus is on human-centred product development, the ethnographic research study design is generally suggested. Methods of qualitative social research such as observational studies and interviews are applied here. Based on the results obtained, problem areas can be identified within the project context. These problem areas are subsequently compared in the literature. After selecting a specific problem which is considered most relevant for the project, design research methods such as cultural probes and design workshops are conducted. The material collected is then evaluated and interpreted. The overall results of this research process are used, on the one hand, to refine the initial research question on which the further practical design work is based and, on the other hand, to summarise and transfer the outcome into a design briefing. The design briefing lists the requirements with regard to the technical, aesthetic, and symbolic design functions that are to be addressed in the project. Furthermore, based on the results of the previous process phases, archetypal users, such as personas, use cases, scenarios, and storyboards, are determined for the project in order to ensure the focus on the target group of the project.

The design briefing resulting from the qualitative research process marks the passage to the applied research process. Within this research process, action research, which can be understood as comparative research, is chosen as the study design. The focus is on researching the conditions and effects of social action, as well as the reflected action within a design process. Although the course of an action research process depends heavily on practical circumstances, there are two steps that must be taken into account. According to Muratovski (2016), a goal or a research question is first defined, followed by an action which is then evaluated. The process is characterised above all by the constant change and the repetition of information collection, analysis, and processing. Preliminary results are implemented and tested in several iterations during the research process. Another criterion of action research is the equal rights of all those involved, which are guaranteed through the constant exchange between researchers and people in the target group (ibid., pp. 190-201).

After the development of design approaches, design studies, and mock-up model building, a selection of the most promising design directions is made. In an iterative process, each design draft is documented, evaluated by the people of the target group, and reflected on with regard to the research question as well as the design briefing. The process is repeated in an iterative approach until the evaluation results convince the future users of the product developed.

The entire research process is completed by a final reflection on the project, starting with reference to the initial research question, the data gathered through a comparative literature analysis to contextualise their own work, and the research findings of the qualitative and applied research process.

Applied Research

conducted by a mixed-methods
(qualitative and applied) research approach

Research
project preparation

- ► selection of project area
- ► preliminary problem definition
- ► preliminary definition of research question
- ► comparative literature analysis
  (for example chronological examination, historical research, thematic analysis, methodological comparison, theoretical comparison, meta-analysis)
- ► comparative analysis of creative works within the selected area with regard to the technical, aesthetic and symbolic design function

User Studies
research process = qualitative research,
study design = ethnographic research

- ► definition of target group
- ► conduction of social scientific research methods for the collection of user, aesthetic, technical, ecological and economic requirements
- ► definition of problem areas, literature review
- ► conduction of design research methods for the collection of user, aesthetic, technical, ecological and economic requirements
- ► analysis of findings = list of overall requirements
- ► refinement of research question
- ► design briefing (technical / aesthetic / symbolic design function)
- ► creation of personas, use-cases, scenarios, storyboards

Design
research process = applied research,
study design = action research

- ► design concept development - 2D and 3D sketches
- ► experiment 1: detailed elaboration of a design draft - documentation "reflection-in-action"
- ► experiment 1: model building - documentation "reflection-in-action"
- ► experiment 1: evaluation with end-users - documentation "reflection-in-action"
- ► experiment 1: documentation of experiment 1 using "reflection-on-action"
- ► repetition of the experiment phase until the final design

Contextualisation

- ► final reflection on the project with reference to the initial research question, the contextualisation through literature, and the research findings of the qualitative and applied research process

Table 9: Overview of the applied research process in design

In the introduction to this publication, we have already pointed out that one of the central questions that research in design must answer is what kind of knowledge is generated by the conduction of the research.

In the process guide we propose here, we argue that due to the use of social scientific research methods, the social reality of people in the target group is investigated in order to identify a problem to be solved. The product designed through the applied research process represents a solution approach to the identified problem. The knowledge generated is therefore not the product designed per se, but the measurable effectiveness in terms of positive change in the social reality of the persons in the target group of the product.

We are aware that the detailed evaluation of the product would exceed the limited time frame of a semester. In line with our intention to familiarise students at the BA level with the holistic design process in terms of linking research and practice, the guide is intended to contribute to the development of basic knowledge on how research can be integrated into design practice. In particular, the contextualisation phase is intended to raise awareness early in design studies that reflection and evaluation of output appropriate to the project's purpose and methodology is the basis for identifying research-related findings in design.

Figure 12: "Pets" project (Photo: Korab)

G2.1 Examples of applied research

This chapter presents two examples of final student projects that we place in the category of applied research. The first project represents the traditional categorisation of the development of a product design after conducting user studies and identifying product-related requirements and needs. The second project is oriented towards applied research as the investigation of a practical application for a specific theoretical concept or approach.

Example 1 - "Pets: objects to support and sit on" by Georg Siegele

The "Pets: objects to support and sit on" project by Georg Siegele is a prime example of how applied research in product design can be implemented from the definition of a project area to a fully functional prototype implemented with the highest level of craftsmanship.

Abstract:
The work is subject to the principles of "Design for Human Diversity". It is important to understand that this term further stands for concepts such as Universal Design, Inclusive Design and Design for All. The project was developed on the basis of the research question: "How can the everyday mobility of people be improved by providing a stand-up and support function?" By stand-up and support functions, the following is meant: support (getting up from somewhere), support (holding on) and half-sitting or standing (sitting position between sitting and standing).

After a certain age, people's muscle strength begins to weaken, their sense of balance is weakened or other limitations occur, but even young people can lose their vitality due to illness or injury. From this point on, people often need products to support their everyday mobility. However, such products are usually designed only under the aspect of functionality and do not take into account stigmatization as well as emotionality.

This work is preceded by my theoretical bachelor thesis (Design for Human Diversity: Meaning and Accessible Application), which can be seen as a theoretical basis for the development of the research question. Practically, observations, research on competing products as well as interviews were conducted, sketches were drawn, 1:1 models were made and tested, and finally prototypes were produced.

The results of the work are exciting designs that appeal emotionally without intervention, offer support to the user, but do not thereby assign him to a population group (stigmatize). The result is not a design for old people, but a design for everyone that works across generations. (Georg Siegele)

Armlehne

breitere oben kürzere
Sitzfläche

Figure 13: Design concept development (Sketches: Siegele)

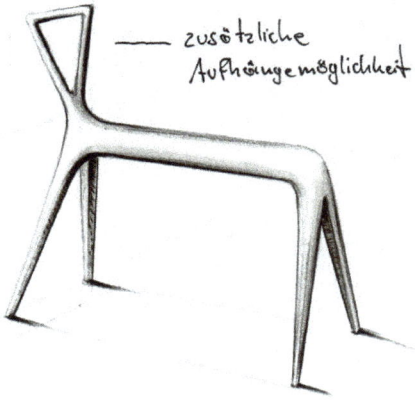

zusätzliche
Aufhängemöglichkeit

2x Armlehne

Winkel mit
Armlehne

115

Figure 14: Project preparation – comparative design analysis (Photo: Siegele)

Figure 15: Evaluation (Photo: Siegele)

Figure 16: Evaluation of the products developed with end users
(Photo: Siegele)

Example 2 - "Meat Plates: deliberately bloody" by Katharina Partik

The "Meat Plates: deliberately bloody" work by Katharina Partik illustrates that the process guide of applied development can also be used in the context of product development for a more conceptually oriented project. The project also shows that elements of experimental development, in this case experimental series for the production of a "blood glaze", can be carried out within the framework of a project defined as applied research, since the process guidelines are not conveyed as dogmatic specifications but as orientation aids and planning tools that must be adapted to the individual objectives of the students.

Abstract:

With reference to the increase in awareness of the enjoyment of high-quality meat, the project answers the question of how this process can be taken into account through an object of table culture such as the plate.

Meat plays a major role in our diet. For many, it plays such an important role that it has become a staple food. However, this is not necessarily a good thing, because it means that we eat too much meat and, above all, too cheap meat. Meat is something special and should only be eaten with a high level of awareness. If we were reminded of the slaughter while eating meat, it would affect our meat consumption. We would be much more present and aware of the meat and reach for better quality. This is what the bachelor project wants to aim at.

Blood plays a major role in the meat plates. Through the blood, the association to death and life and thus to slaughter should be awakened, whereby the meat should be eaten more consciously. Through a series of experiments, a blood glaze was developed, which is characterized by a structure. In addition, a blood groove was incorporated, in which the bloody meat juice of the steak is to collect during the meal.

In this way, an object of table culture such as the plate raises awareness for the enjoyment of high-quality meat. (Katharina Partik)

Figure 17: "Meat Plates" project (Photo: Korab)

Figure 18: "Meat Plates" project – plate only (Photo: Korab)

Figure 19: Project preparation
(Photos: top – Natalie Zipfl, „Blood leather"; bottom – Basse Stittgen, „Blood Related")

Figure 20: Experiment (Photo: Partik)

Process guidelines

Figure 21: Experiment (Photo: Partik)

Figure 22: Design concept development (Illustration: Partik)

G3   Experimental development

As with the applied research process, the research activity of experimental development requires project preparation and the individual steps in it are congruent. After the project preparation and to meet the requirements of the systematic investigation, a study plan of the individual experiments is first developed. Each experiment is described based on the factor that is being investigated, how and where it is being investigated, and who is involved in the investigation. In addition, the documentation of each experiment follows the process of implementation, observation, and evaluation.

The question of how academic research can be conducted within individual creative practice has been discussed intensively in academia in the past decades. Mäkelä and Nimkulrat (2018) presented the approach of using documentation as a support tool for the reflection process on practical design work and showcased three dissertation projects in the realms of ceramics, glass, and textiles as case studies which were carried out at Aalto University in Finland. With these case studies, they wanted to examine the role of documentation in practice-based research projects with regard to the possibilities of communicating, capturing, and understanding experimental knowledge.

Concerning the reflection process within practical design work, they used the approach of the reflective practitioner which was developed by social scientist Donald Schön in 1991. The authors stated that Schön had divided the possibilities for reflection on practical design work into the time during the design process, for example, the reflection-in-action, and the time after the design process, for example, the reflection-on-action (ibid., p. 2).

In addition to the different nature of the three areas in which the dissertation projects took place, ceramics, glass, and textiles, and the different research processes which were chosen for these projects, it was found that two types of documentation were used for the reflection-in and on-action. On the one hand, there is "documentation of making of the artefacts" (ibid., p. 12), which takes place during the design process and can be implemented both visually and textually, and on the other hand, there is "documentation for making the artefacts" (ibid., p. 12), which takes place before the design action while the designer is still looking for inspiration.

In summary, the reflection-in-action method was used to collect information about the creative process and the reflection-on-action method was used to analyse the information about the creative process. In all three cases, the results of the documentation were contextualised with relevant literature after the design process. The authors concluded that documentation of and reflection on the creative process were necessary for the development of a practice-based doctorate in art and design.

Experimental Development

conducted by a mixed-methods (qualitative and applied) research approach

Research
project preparation

- ► selection of project area
- ► preliminary problem definition
- ► preliminary definition of research question
- ► comparative literature analysis (for example chronological examination, historical research, thematic analysis, methodological comparison, theoretical comparison, meta-analysis)
- ► comparative analysis of creative works within the selected area

Material Research
research process = applied research,
study design = action research

- ► development of study plan
- ► experiment 1: detailed description of the object of investigation (what?, why?, how?, where?, who?)
- ► experiment 1: experiment conduction - documentation "reflection-in-action"
- ► experiment 1: experiment observation - documentation "reflection-in-action"
- ► experiment 1: experiment evaluation – documentation "reflection-on-action"
- ► repetition of the experiment phase until the final design

Design
research process = applied research,
study design = action research

- ► design concept development - 2D and 3D sketches
- ► experiment 1: detailed elaboration of a design draft - documentation "reflection-in-action"
- ► experiment 1: model building - documentation "reflection-in-action"
- ► experiment 1: evaluation with end-users - documentation "reflection-in-action"
- ► experiment 1: documentation of experiment 1 using "reflection-on-action"
- ► repetition of the experiment phase until the final design

Contextualisation
- ► final reflection on the project with reference to the initial research question, the contextualisation through literature, and the results of the experiments conducted

Table 10: Overview of the experimental development reserach process in design

An interesting detail regarding the process of the individual case studies is that each of the three projects had gone through an iterative design process. After determining the topic and the question to be investigated, each of the projects was initially researched. For each project and in three successive iterations, objects were designed, built, and presented in an exhibition. Each iteration was carried out using the documentation method of reflection-in and on-action (ibid.). The process methodology used is interesting in terms of consistency with the study design of action research.

As already described in the research process for applied research, this process also closes with the final reflection on the experiments carried out and the contextualisation with the existing literature.

As earlier explained in the chapter on applied research, we would like to return briefly to the question of what knowledge is generated by the proposed process guide for experimental development. By using research methods in accordance with engineering and the natural sciences, a problem to be solved is also identified here, which is investigated by conducting the series of experiments with the aim of finding a solution for it. The application example designed through the research process of experimental development represents a solution approach for the identified problem. The knowledge generated through this process therefore again does not refer to the designed application example per se, but to the measurable technical properties of the material developed.

G3.1 Examples of experimental development

In contrast to the student projects presented in the chapter on applied research, the following projects are not characterised by the objective of concrete product development, but rather by experimental research on materials and tools. The artefacts and prototypes that are shown as results serve in this case primarily as means for communicating the research results of the projects and their possible fields of application.

Figure 23: "Nux" project (Photo: Korab)

Example 3 - "Nux: Walnut(shell) Material Study" by Katharina Meixner

Abstract:

Walnut shell is a natural, renewable and degradable waste material from the food industry, which is mainly burned. However, the shell is a raw material that offers unique technical and experiential properties. Based on this, this paper addresses the research question of how and what materials can be produced from the walnut shell and what properties they possess. To answer the research question, a theoretical basis on walnut (shell) is first established and explored through practical material experiments.

In order to counteract the drastically advancing climate change, renewable and biodegradable materials should be used more than ever, but they must not only withstand technical requirements. The "immaterial spark" they give off is essential in order to be accepted by the users. Through experimentation and the designers' engagement with the material, completely new, unique and aesthetic material creations can emerge, which incorporate the ecological and technical aspects from the outset and, above all, take into account the emotional bond between people and material.

The result of this work is a material that ultimately uses the whole walnut and does not require any chemical additives. The material is produced by pressure and heat, resulting in a solid, durable material that can be experienced through all the senses. In the end, an object with representative and symbolic character was created. (Katharina Meixner)

Figure 24: Experiment (Photo: Meixner)

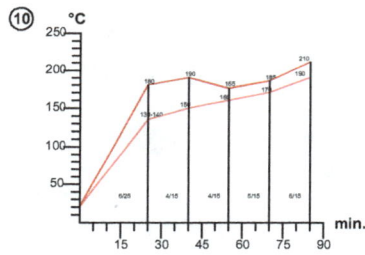

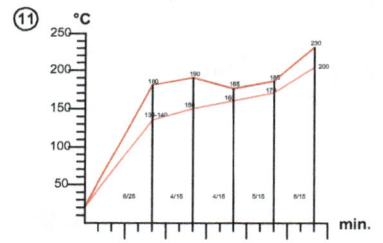

Figure 25: Experiment (Photo: Meixner)

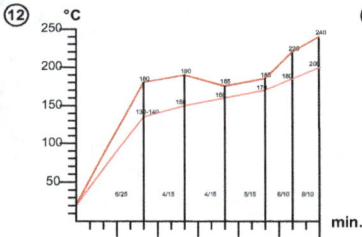

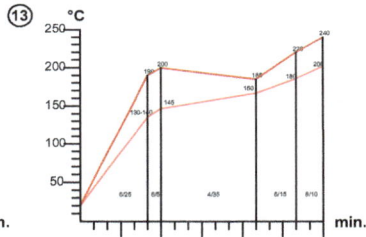

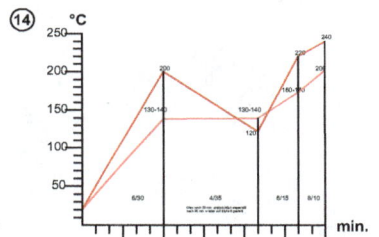

Process guidelines

Figure 26: Experiment (Photo: Korab)

Example 4 - "3D printing as a tool?" by Dennis Paulus

"3D printing as a tool?" by Dennis Paulus explores the extent to which practical know how in the use of a numerically controlled production tool can open up new possibilities for design.

Abstract:
How can the tool 3D printing be handled correctly from a technological and aesthetic point of view and how can the potential of the technology be exploited? The aim is to identify and practically explore special techniques and applications of 3D FDM printing in order to be able to handle it correctly and to design objects and/or products on the basis of it. The tool used is therefore a 3D printer of the FDM family (Fused Deposition Modeling). The created things should be able to express this special approach with the tool 3D printer by means of their appearance.

Design is not only a question of the finished product, but also of the practical and theoretical background. This bachelor thesis works on the theoretical symbol "3D printer tool" on a practical level, by means of experiments and research with and around this device. (Dennis Paulus)

Figure 27: "3D printing as a tool?" project (Photo: Paulus)
Figure 28: Result of experiment (Photo: Paulus)

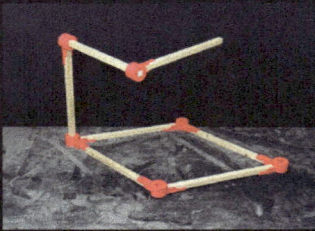

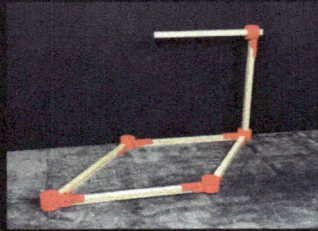

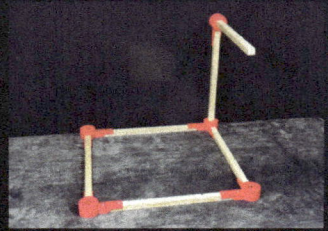

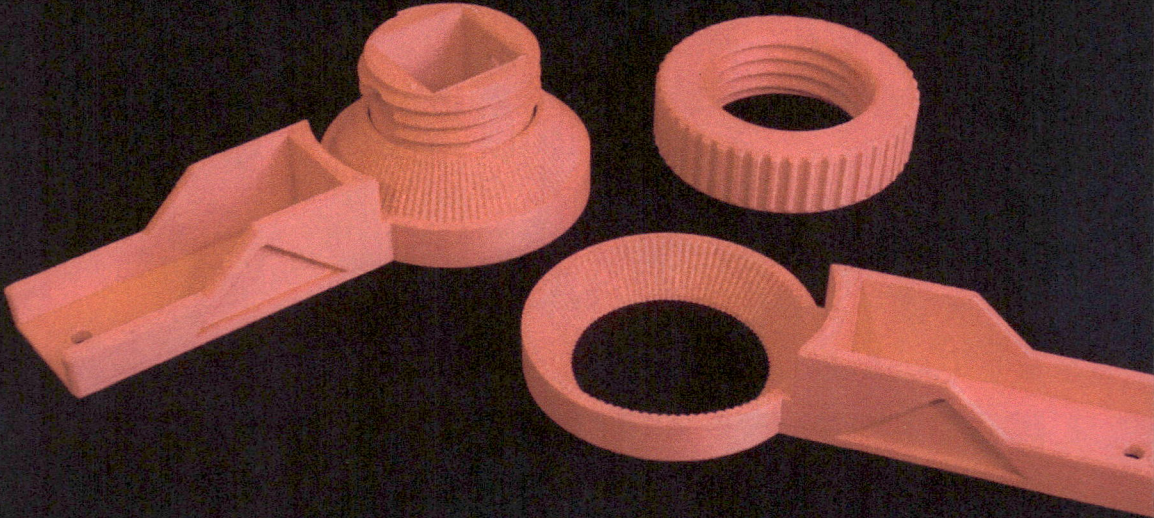

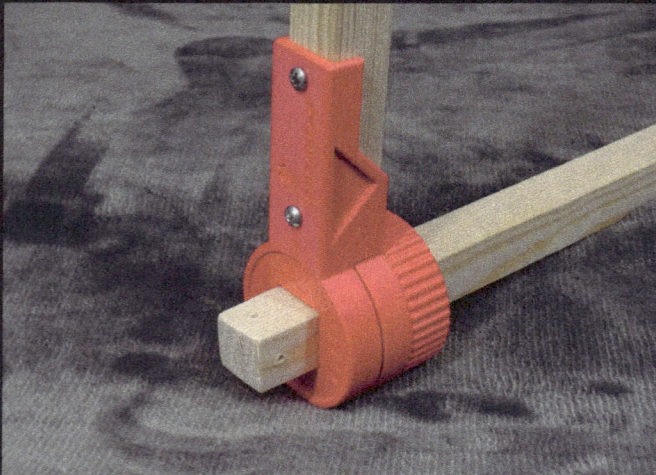

Figure 29: 3D printed variable connection module for furniture construction
Semester project, Dennis Paulus 2020 (Photo: Paulus)

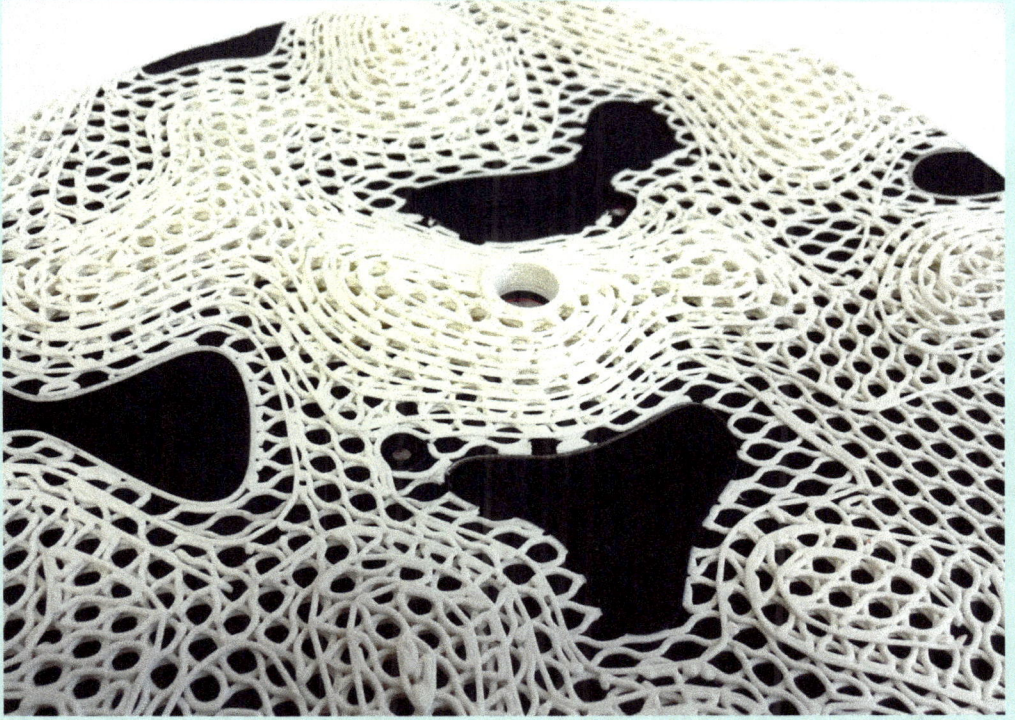

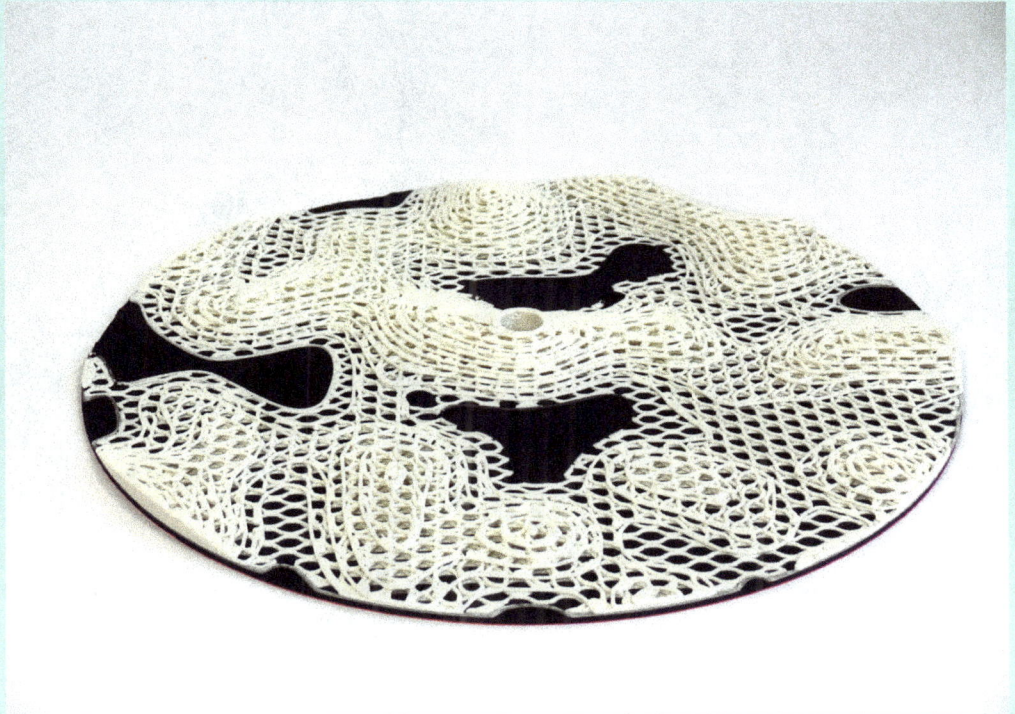

Figure 30: Experiment (Photo: Paulus)

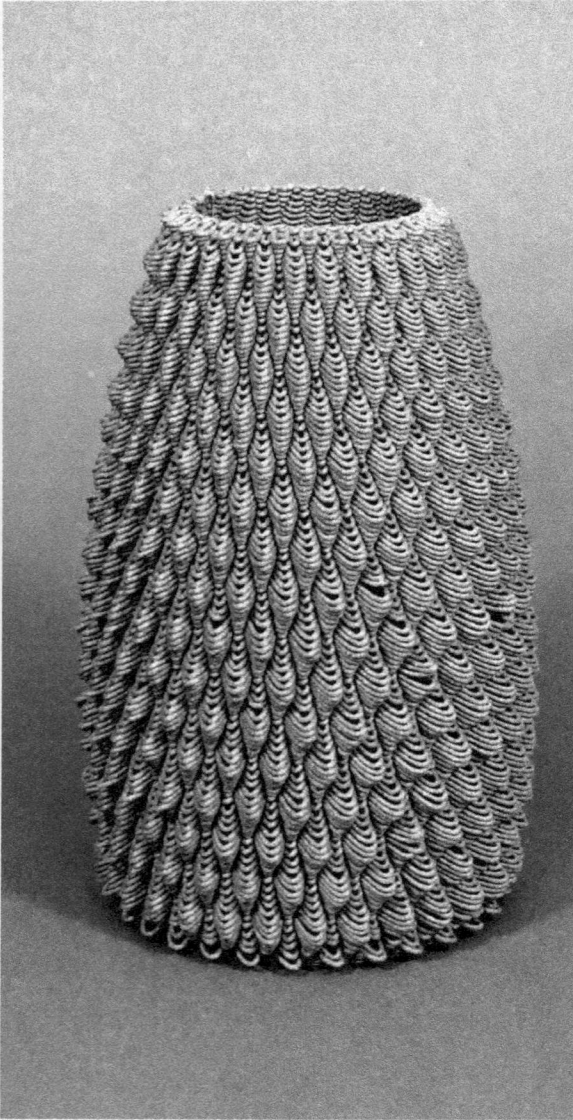

Figure 31: Experiment (Photo: Paulus)

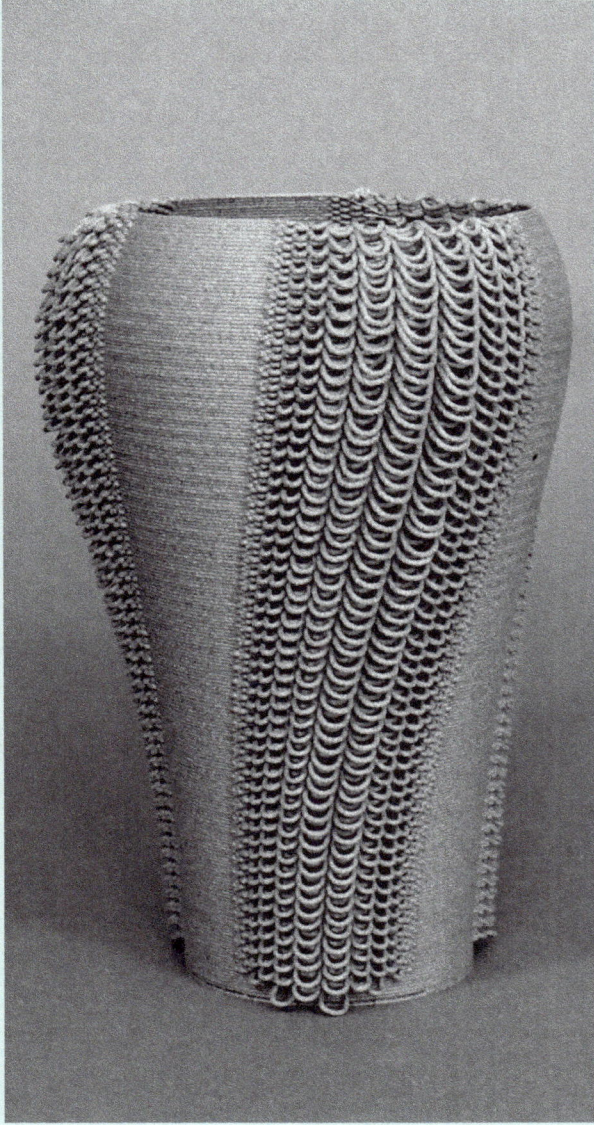

Figure 32: Result of experiment (Photo: Paulus)

Teaching Research in Design

G4   Contextualisation / reflection

With reference once again to the two process guidelines presented, the last point of contextualisation should be addressed here. As can already be seen from the respective sequence of the process phases, this point is specifically intended to promote the students' ability to contextualise the work they created with regard to the relevant literature, comparable products or materials, the findings from the user studies or the material research, up to the solution approach they developed in the form of a product or a material application.

However, there is usually no time for reflection on the research results and the course of the project in the daily routine of design practice. The closer the end of the project or the presentation date, the more attention must be paid to questions of practical implementation, and after a more or less successful presentation, the next project usually already follows.

But especially the analysis of the development process based on its documentation and the evaluation of the concrete design outputs is essential for the identification of research-related project results. We therefore advocate that contextualisation and reflection be cultivated as an integral part of the design process from the very beginning of design education.

To this end, we believe it is essential to schedule the project conclusion not with the presentation or submission of the design results and its documentation, as is generally the case, but with a few days' interval and to include a written summary of the main findings from the project and the feedback on the results by target groups and experts. ◄

H   Discussion

After completing the studies and developing the process guides in the RIDE research project, it became clear to us that this is really just the beginning or the first step of actually approaching design teaching for the integration of research in design practice.

As a first realisation, it became apparent that the endeavour inevitably also entails a serious restructuring of design studio teaching as it is currently practised. As mentioned in previous chapters, it became obvious that in order to implement the plan to teach a holistic design process of research and design practice, a teaching staff in the design studio consisting of teachers who cover the areas of research and practice is absolutely necessary. This represents a clear change from the current practice so far, since only designers usually supervise students in this course.

The necessity of restructuring the curriculum with regard to the integration of research in the design process is also reflected in the didactic concept presented in chapter E. We described that the students received specific theoretical input about the design process methodologies and design research methods they could use to support their work. They were assisted by lecture notes, providing details on the two process methodologies as well as a variety of research methods for each phase of a holistic design process, and a process documentation InDesign template which they were to fill in so that by the end of the semester, they would not only present a final practical project, but have a written documentation (including literature reviews, research findings, design process, photos, etc.) of their project.

As a reflection on the didactic concept, the teaching materials produced, and the guides developed, it is noted that the students seem to be fundamentally clear about the difference between the design research processes for either product development or material development. However, it must also be stated that they have difficulties with the research terminology used, such as methodology, study design, method, and methodology. Since during the studies conducted within our research project, the students only came into contact with this new language of research in their third year of study, they were partly overwhelmed by the task of learning the new language at the same time as working on their projects. It is a big step to move away from the familiar image of research in design, which is actually conducted more or less as a form of exploration, for example, by collecting images for mood boards, compiling cultural probes packages, or even informally interviewing people, to prepare students for the next level of conducting design research according to scientific standards. The level of detail and the necessary verifiability of the methods used pose not inconsiderable challenges for many students. As a conclusion, the training in terms of terminology and methodological knowledge must take place from the first semester onwards. In addition, the preparation, implementation, documentation, and reflection of research methods should be practised from the beginning. It is important to dispel the myth that research is rigorous, non-creative, and far removed from practical translatability. Therefore, it should be emphasised that photos should still be taken, for example, of the project context, material samples should be collected, and design mock-ups should be built.

Design research according to scientific standards does not have to be less colourful, free, or creative. The main difference that can be identified is the level of detail to the methodological foundations of what one does and the connection of the research results to other disciplines. Learning a new language, however, affects not only design students but, at least to the same extent, design educators within a degree programme. As explained in chapter B, there are a variety of definitions and interpretations of research in design. Therefore, in order for students to sustainably learn how to integrate research into their practical design work, it is essential that there is consensus among a faculty and the teaching staff on the chosen research definition, research processes, and terminology.

In addition to all the knowledge we have been able to gain through the intensive examination of this topic and the insights we have made through the studies conducted, the real core of the discussion about the definition of what is considered research in design and how it is integrated into design work is presented by the fusion of two different positions. The relationship between design and research is not unencumbered. Rather, it is a history of mutual prejudices and stereotypes. On the one hand, designers complain about the limitations and lack of allowed creativity they often associate with research work, and on the other hand, researchers complain about the lack of verifi-ability of methods, contextualisation of results, and orientation towards traditional scientific standards in general. As mentioned in the last chapter, we see research work as an integral part of the creative process, which in no way competes with the design work, but rather supports it with orientation, structure, traceability, and connectivity to traditional scientific disciplines. Bringing these two positions together is an enormous task that can only be achieved through openness, a willingness to experiment, and a thirst for knowledge on the part of all those involved. ◄

I References

Almendra, Rita A. and Ferreira, João (2020) REDES – The vision for a research group on research & education in design. In: Almendra, Rita A. and Ferreire, João [eds.]: *Research & Education in Design: People & Processes & Products & Philosophy. Proceedings of the 1st International Conference on Research and Education.* London: Taylor & Francis, pp. 197-203. https://doi.org/10.1201/9781003046103-22

Allpress, Brent (2012) Pedagogical Practices for Supervising Research by Project in Architecture and Design. In: Allpress, Brent, Barnacle, Robyn, Duxbury, Lesley and Grierson, Elizabeth [eds.]: *Supervising Practices for Postgraduate Research in Art, Architecture and Design.* Rotterdam, Boston: Sense Publishers, pp. 25-39. https://doi.org/10.1007/978-94-6209-019-4_3

Allpress, Brent, Barnacle, Robyn, Duxbury, Lesley and Grierson, Elizabeth (2012) Supervising Practice-led Research by Project in Art, Creative Writing, Architecture and Design. In: Allpress, Brent, Barnacle, Robyn, Duxbury, Lesley and Grierson, Elizabeth [eds.]: *Supervising Practices for Postgraduate Research in Art, Architecture and Design.* Rotterdam, Boston: Sense Publishers, pp. 1-14. https://doi.org/10.1007/978-94-6209-019-4_1

Allpress, Brent and Barnacle, Robyn (2012) [eds.]: *Supervising Practices for Postgraduate Research in Art, Architecture and Design.* Rotterdam, Boston: Sense Publishers.

Archer, Bruce (1979) Design as a Discipline. In: *Design Studies*, Vol. 1, No. 1, pp. 18-20. https://doi.org/10.1016/0142-694X(79)90023-1

Archer, Bruce (1995) The Nature of Research. In: *Co-design, interdisciplinary journal of design*, pp. 6-13.

Badura, Jens, Dubach, Selma, Haarmann, Anke, Mersch, Dieter, Rey, Anton, Schenker, Christoph & Toro-Pérez, Germán (2015) *Künstlerische Forschung. Ein Handbuch.* Zürich: diaphanes. https://doi.org/10.4472/9783037345832

Badura, Jens, Dubach, Selma and Haarmann, Anke (2015) Vorweg: Warum ein Handbuch zur künstlerischen Forschung. In: Badura, Jens, Dubach, Selma, Haarmann, Anke, Mersch, Dieter, Rey, Anton, Schenker, Christoph and Toro Pérez, Germán [eds.]: *Künstlerische Forschung. Ein Handbuch.* 1. Aufl. Zürich: Diaphanes, pp. 9-16. https://doi.org/10.4472/9783037345832.0001

Bayazit, Nigan (2004) Investigating Design: A Review of Forty Years of Design Research. In: *Design Issues*, Vol. 20, No. 1, Winter 2004, pp. 16-29. https://doi.org/10.1162/074793604772933739

Biggs, Michael A. R. (2002) The role of the artefact in art and design research. In: *International Journal of Design Sciences and Technology*, Vol. 10, No. 2, pp. 19-24.

Blythe, Richard and Stamm, Marcelo (2019) Doctoral Training for Practitioners: ADAPTR (Architecture, Design and Art Practice Research) A European Commission Marie Curie Initial Training Network. In: Vaughan, Laurene [ed.]: *Practice-based Design Research.* London, New York, Oxford, New Delhi, Sydney: Bloomsbury, pp. 52-63.

Bohnsack, Ralf (2006) Die dokumentarische Methode der Bildinterpretation in der Forschungspraxis. In: Marotzki, Winfried and Niesyto, Horst [eds.]: *Bildinterpretation und Bildverstehen: Methodische Ansätze aus sozialwissenschaftlicher, kunst- und medienpädagogischer Perspektive.* Wiesbaden: Springer.

Bonsiepe, Gui (2009) Entwurf und Entwurfsforschung. Differenz und Affinität [Design and design research. Difference and affinity]. In: Bonsiepe, Gui [ed.]: *Entwurfskultur und Gesellschaft. Gestaltung zwischen Zentrum und Peripherie* [Design culture and society. Design between centrum and periphery]. Zürich, Switzerland: Zürcher Hochschule der Künste und Birkhäuser, pp. 199-218. https://doi.org/10.1007/978-3-0346-0389-8_12

Brandes, Uta, Erlhoff, Michael and Schemann, Nadine (2009) *Designtheorie und Designforschung.* Paderborn: Fink. https://doi.org/10.36198/9783838531526

Brandes, Sven and Schaefer, Ina (2013) Partizipative Evaluation in Praxisprojekten. Chancen und Herausforderungen. In: *Prävention und Gesundheitsförderung*, 8, S. 132–137.

Brandt, Eva and Binder, Thomas (2007) Experimental design research: genealogy, intervention, argument [online]. Available at: https://www.sd.polyu.edu.hk/iasdr/proceeding/papers/Experimental%20design%20research_%20genealogy%20-%20intervention%20-%20argument.pdf (accessed 29.06.2022).

Braun, Edith, Gusy, Burkhard, Leidner, Bernard and Hannover, Bettina (2008) Das Berliner Evaluationsinstrument für selbsteingeschätzte, studentische Kompetenzen (BEvaKomp). In: *DIAGNOSTICA*, Vol. 54, No. 1, pp. 30-42. https://doi.org/10.1026/0012-1924.54.1.30

Brew, Angela (2013) Understanding the scope of undergraduate research: a framework for curricular and pedagogical decision-making. In: *Higher Education*, Vol. 66, No. 5, pp. 603-618. https://doi.org/10.1007/s10734-013-9624-x

Candy, Linda (2006) *Practice Based Research: A Guide.* CCS Report: 2006-V1.0 November, University of Technology Sydney [online]. Available at: https://www.creativityandcognition.com/resources/PBR%20 Guide-1.1-2006.pdf (accessed 29.06.2022).

Candy, Linda and Edmonds, Ernest (2018) Practice-Based Research in the Creative Arts. Foundations and Futures from the Front Line. In: *Leonardo*, Vol. 51, No. 1, pp. 63-69. https://doi.org/10.1162/LEON_a_01471

Cash, Philip J. (2018) Developing theory-driven design research. In: *Design Studies*, Vol. 56, pp. 84-119. https://doi.org/10.1016/j.destud.2018.03.002

Clemente, Violeta, Tschimmel, Katja and Pombo, Lúcia (2020) Mapping the territories around Design Research: A four-layer analysis. In: Almendra, Rita A. and Ferreira, João [eds.]: *Research & Education in Design: People & Processes & Products & Philosophy. Proceedings of the 1st International Conference on Research and Education.* London: Taylor & Francis, pp. 147-156. https://doi.org/10.1201/9781003046103-17

Cross, Nigel (1982) Designerly ways of knowing. In: *Design Studies*, Vol. 3, No. 4, pp. 221-227. https://doi.org/10.1016/0142-694X(82)90040-0

Cumulus International Association of Universities and Colleges of Art, Design and Media (2019) Cumulus conference Rovaniemi 2019 Around the Campfire: Resilience and Intelligence [online]. Available at https://cumulusassociation.org/events/cumulus-conferences/around-the-campfire-resilience-and-intelligence/ (accessed 29.06.2022).

Dalton, Ben, Simmons, Tom and Triggs, Teal (2019) Knowledge Exchange through the Design PhD. In: Vaughan, Laurene [ed.]: *Practice-based Design Research.* London, New York, Oxford, New Delhi, Sydney: Bloomsbury, pp. 65-76.

Daxer, Elisabeth (2019) Künstlerische Forschung – Artistic Research. In: Hug, Theo, Niedermair, Klaus and Drexler, Arthur [eds.]: Wissenschaftliches Arbeiten. *Eine Handreichung.* 4., erweiterte und überarbeitete Auflage. Innsbruck: Studia Verlag, pp. 150-155.

De Freitas, Nancy (2002) Towards a Definition of Studio Documentation: working tool and transparent record. In: *Working Papers in Art and Design*, 2 [online]. Available at: https://www.herts.ac.uk/__data/assets/pdf_file/0011/12305/WPIAAD_vol2_freitas.pdf (accessed 29.06.2022).

De Freitas, Nancy (2007) Activating a Research Context in Art and Design Practice. In: *International Journal for the Scholarship of Teaching and Learning*, Vol. 1, No. 2, Art. 14. https://doi.org/10.20429/ijsotl.2007.010214

Deignan, Tim (2009) Enquiry-Based Learning: perspectives on practice. In: *Teaching in Higher Education*, Vol. 14, No. 1, pp. 13-28. https://doi.org/10.1080/13562510802602467

Didion, Denise and Wiemer, Matthias (2009) Forschendes Lernen als interdisziplinäres Element des Studium Fundamentale. In: *Journal Hochschuldidaktik*, Vol. 20, No. 2, pp. 7-9.

Diekmann, Andreas (2007) *Empirische Sozialforschung.* Reinbek: Rowohlt.

Dittenberger, Sandra (2018) Putting Theory to Practice: Reflections on the Integration of Product Design Aspects in AAL Projects. In: Marjanović, Dorian, Štorga, Mario, Škec, Stanko, Bojčetić, Nenad and Pavković, Neven [eds.] *Proceedings of the 15th International Design Conference DESIGN 2018.* Dubrovnik: Croatia. https://doi.org/10.21278/idc.2018.0187

Dittenberger, Sandra (2019) Actively reflective: understanding the drivers and hurdles of building knowledge bridges between theory and practice in design education. In: Häkkilä, Jonna, Pakanen, Minna, Luiro, Elina, Mikkonen, Enni and Miettinen, Satu [eds.]: *Cumulus Conference Proceedings Series 5/2019: Around the Campfire – Resilience and Intelligence.* Rovaniemi: Cumulus: International Association of Universities and Colleges of Art, Design and Media.

Dorst, Kees (2013) *Academic design* [online]. Available at: http://alexandria.tue.nl/extra2/redes/dorst2013.pdf (accessed 29.06.2022).

Downton, Peter (2012) Beside Myself: Scrutinising Decades of Supervising Designers. In: Allpress, Brent, Barnacle, Robyn, Duxbury, Lesley and Grierson, Elizabeth [eds.]: *Supervising Practices for Postgraduate Research in Art*, Architecture and Design. Rotterdam, Boston: Sense Publishers, pp. 117-130. https://doi.org/10.1007/978-94-6209-019-4_10

Dürnberger, Hannah (2014) *Forschendes Lernen unter Einsatz digitaler Medien beim Verfassen der Bachelorarbeit – Potenziale für die Schlüsselkompetenzentwicklung.* Dissertation: Zeppelin Universität.

Dunin-Woyseth, Halina and Nilsson, Frederik (2014) Design Education, Practice, and Research: on building a field of inquiry. In: *Studies in Material Thinking*, Vol. 11, pp. 3-17 [online]. Available at: http://publications.lib.chalmers.se/records/fulltext/202140/local_202140.pdf (accessed 29.06.2022).

Duxbury, Robyn (2012) Opening the Door. Portals to Good Supervision of Creative Practice-led Research. In: Allpress, Brent, Barnacle, Robyn, Duxbury, Lesley and Grierson, Elizabeth [eds.]: *Supervising Practices for Postgraduate Research in Art, Architecture and Design.* Rotterdam, Boston: Sense Publishers, pp. 15-21. https://doi.org/10.1007/978-94-6209-019-4_2

Ehn, Pelle and Ullmark, Peter (2019) Educating the Reflective Designer. In: Vaughan, Laurene [ed.]: *Practice-based Design Research.* London, New York, Oxford, New Delhi, Sydney: Bloomsbury, pp. 77-86.

Fachhochschule Potsdam (2019) Fachbereich Design [online]. Available at: https://www.fh-potsdam.de/design/ (accessed 29.06.2022).

Findeli, Alain (1998) A Quest for Credibility: Doctoral Education and Research in Design at the University of Montreal. In: *Proceedings of the Ohio Conference on Doctoral Education in Design*, Ohio, Oct. 8-11, 1998, pp. 99-116.

Fink, Corinna (2010) Kompetenzorientierte Lehrevaluation. Diskussion neuer Perspektiven für neue Lehr- und Lern-formen. *Lern-Service-Engineering*. Multikonferenz Wirtschaftsinformatik, 23.-25.02.2010 (pp. 433-444), Göttingen, Germany: Georg-August-Universität [online]. Available at: http://webdoc.sub.gwdg.de/univerlag/2010/mkwi/01_management_und_methoden/lern-service-engineering/07_kompetenzorientierte_lehrevaluation.pdf (accessed 29.06.2022).

FL² Forschendes Lernen – Lehrende Forschung Fachhochschule Potsdam [ed.] (2015) Formen Forschenden Lernens an der Fachhochschule Potsdam. 2. Aufl. [online]. Available at: https://ecampus.fh-potsdam.de/pluginfile.php/283967/mod_resource/content/1/Beispiel_Literatur2.pdf (accessed 29.06.2022).

Flick, Uwe (2009) *Sozialforschung: Methoden und Anwendungen. Ein Überblick für die BA-Studiengänge.* Reinbek bei Hamburg: Rowohlt Taschenbuch Verlag.

Frascara, Jorge (2007) Hiding Lack of Knowledge: Bad Words in Design Education. In: *Design Issues*, Vol. 23, No. 4, pp. 62-68. https://doi.org/10.1162/desi.2007.23.4.62

Frayling, Chrisopher (1993) Research in Art and Design. In: *Royal College of Art Research Papers*, Vol. 1, No. 1, pp. 1-5.

Friedman, Ken (2003) Theory Construction in Design Research Criteria. In: *Design Studies*, Vol. 24, No. 6, pp. 507-522. https://doi.org/10.1016/S0142-694X(03)00039-5

Friedman, Ken (2017) PhD in Art and Design. In: *Leonardo*, Vol. 50, No. 5, pp. 515-519. https://doi.org/10.1162/LEON_e_01472

Fromm, Martin (2012) *Beobachtung. Anleitung und Übung*. Norderstedt: Books on Demand.

Gelmez, Kory (2017) Towards a taxonomy of design learning based on students' reflective writings. *REDO Cumulus Design Conference 2017, 30.05–02.06.2017*. Kolding, Denmark: Design School Kolding.

Hanington, Bruce. M. (2010) Relevant and Rigorous: Human Centered Research and Design Education. In: *Design Issues*, Vol. 26, No. 3, Summer 2010, pp. 18-26. https://doi.org/10.1162/DESI_a_00026

Healey, Mick and Jenkins, Alan (2009) *Developing undergraduate research and inquiry*. The Higher Education Academy [online]. Available at: https://www.heacademy.ac.uk/knowledge-hub/developing-undergraduate-research-and-inquiry (accessed 29.06.2022).

Herriott, Richard (2019) What kind of research is research through design? Proceedings of the International Association of Societies of Design Research Conference 2019, Manchester School of Art, Manchester Metropolitan University, 2-5 September 2019, pp. 2-11 [online]. Available at: https://iasdr2019.org/uploads/files/Proceedings/op-f-1078-Her-R.pdf (accessed 29.06.2022).

Hockey, John (2008) Practice-based Research Degree Students in Art and Design: Identity and Adaptation. In: Hickman, Richard [ed.]: *Research in art and design education: issues and exemplars*. Bristol, UK, Chicago: Intellect, pp. 109-119.

Huber, Ludwig (2013) Warum Forschendes Lernen nötig und möglich ist. In: Huber, Ludwig, Hellmer, Julia and Schneider, Friederike [eds.]: *Forschendes Lernen im Studium*. Bielefeld: Universitätsverlag Webler, pp. 9-35. https://doi.org/10.5771/9783845236605-59

Huber, Ludwig (2014) Forschungsbasiertes, Forschungsorientiertes, Forschendes Lernen: Alles dasselbe? Ein Plädoyer für eine Verständigung über Begriffe und Unterscheidungen im Feld forschungsnahen Lehrens und Lernens. In: *Das Hochschulwesen*, Vol. 62, pp. 22-29.

Hohl, Michael (2020) *Wissenschaftliches Arbeiten in Kunst, Design und Architektur: Kriterien für praxisgeleitete Ph.D.-Forschung*. Berlin: DOM publishers.

Höök, Kristina and Löwgren, Jonas (2012) Strong concepts: Intermediate-Level Knowledge in Interaction Design. In: *ACM Transactions on Computer-Human Interaction*, Vol. 19, No. 3, pp. 1-18. https://doi.org/10.1145/2362364.2362371

Jonas, Wolfgang (2004) Forschung durch Design. In: *Tagung des Swiss Design Network*, Basel/CH, 05/2004.

Klebesadel, Helen and Kornetsky, Lisa (2009) Critique as Signature Pedagogy in the Arts. In: Gurung, Regan A. R., Chick, Nancy L. and Haynie, Aeron [eds.]: *Exploring Signature Pedagogies: Approaches to Teaching Disciplinary Habits of Mind*. Sterling, VA: Stylus, pp. 99-117.

Koskinen, Ilpo and Krogh, Peter Gall (2015) Design accountability: When design research entangles theory and practice. In: *International Journal of Design*, Vol. 9, No. 1, pp. 121-127.

Koskinen, Ilpo, Zimmerman, John, Binder, Thomas, Redström, Johan and Wensveen, Stephan (2011) *Design research through practice: From lab, field, and showroom*. San Francisco: Morgan Kaufmann. https://doi.org/10.1016/B978-0-12-385502-2.00005-5

Krogh, Peter Gall and Koskinen, Ilpo (2020) *Drifting by Intention: Four Epistemic Traditions from within Constructive Design Research*. Cham: Springer International Publishing. https://doi.org/10.1007/978-3-030-37896-7

Kruskal, William H. and Wallis, W. Allen (2012) Use of Ranks in One-Criterion Variance Analysis. In: *Journal of the American Statistical Association*, Vol. 47, No. 260, 583-621. https://doi.org/10.1080/01621459.1952.10483441

Langer, Constanze and Schröder, Tobias (2016) Eine aus FL²- und InterFlex-Lehre abgeleitete Idee für ein digitales, interdisziplinäres „Studium Quaerendum". In: FL² Forschendes Lernen – Lehrende Forschung an der Fachhochschule Potsdam [ed.]: *Vom Quadrat zum Format. Forschendes Lernen – Lehrende Forschung an der Fachhochschule Potsdam*, pp. 143-148 [online]. Available at: https://opus4.kobv.de/opus4-fhpotsdam/files/1166/fl2_publikation_vomquadratzumformat_web.pdf (accessed 29.06.2022).

Mäkelä, Maarit Anna and Nimkurlat, Nithikul (2018) Documentation as a practice-led research tool for reflexion on experimental knowledge. In: *FormAkademisk*, Vol. 11, Nr. 2, Art. 5, pp. 1-16. https://doi.org/10.7577/formakademisk.1818

Mareis, Claudia (2010) Designforschung. In: Carduff, Corina, Siegenthaler, Fiona and Wälchli, Tan [eds.]: *Kunst und künstlerische Forschung*. Zürich: Scheidegger & Spiess, pp. 98-107.

Mooraj, Margrit and Pape, Annika (2015) Forschendes Lernen. In: Hochschulrektorenkonferenz [ed.]: *nexus Impulse für die Praxis* 8 [online]. Available at: https://www.hrk-nexus.de/fileadmin/redaktion/hrk-nexus/07-Downloads/07-02-Publikationen/impuls_Forschendes_Lernen.pdf (accessed 29.06.2022).

Muratovski, Gjoko (2016) *Research for designers: a guide to methods and practice*. London: Sage.

OECD (2015) Frascati Manual 2015: *Guidelines for Collecting and Reporting Data on Research and Experimental Development, The Measurement of Scientific, Technological and Innovation Activities*. OECD Publishing: Paris.

Paechter, Manuela, Maier, Brigitte, Dorfer, Alexandra, Salmhofer, Gudrun and Sindler, Alexandra (2007) Kompetenzen als Qualitätskriterien für universitäre Lehre. In: Kluge, A. (Ed.), *Qualitätssicherung und -entwicklung an Hochschulen: Methoden und Ergebnisse*. Lengerich: Pabst Science Publishers, pp. 83-94.

Phillips, Estelle M. and Pugh, Derek Salman (2005) *How to get a PhD: a handbook for students and their supervisors*. Maidenhead: Open Univ. Press.

Prochner, Isabel and Godin, Danny (2022) Quality in research through design projects: Recommendations for evaluation and enhancement. In: *Design Studies*, Vol. 78. https://doi.org/10.1016/j.destud.2021.101061

Prytula, Michael (2016) Mobiles Wohnen. Von der Idee zum realisierungsreifen Prototypen. In: FL² Forschendes Lernen – Lehrende Forschung an der Fachhochschule Potsdam [ed.]: *Vom Quadrat zum Format. Forschendes Lernen – Lehrende Forschung an der Fachhochschule Potsdam*, pp. 81-85 [online]. Available at: https://opus4.kobv.de/opus4-fhpotsdam/files/1166/fl2_publikation_vomquadratzumformat_web.pdf (accessed 29.06.2022).

Riewerts, Kerrin, Weiss, Petra, Wimmelmann, Susanne, Saunders, Constanze, Beyerlin, Simone, Gotzen, Susanne, Linnartz, Dagmar, Thiem, Janina and Gess, Christopher (2018) Forschendes Lernen entdecken, entwickeln, erforschen und evaluieren. In: *die hochschullehre Interdisziplinäre Zeitschrift für Studium und Lehre*, Vol. 4, pp. 389-406 [online]. Available at: http://www.hochschullehre.org/wp-content/files/die_hochschullehre_2018_Riewerts-etal.pdf (accessed 29.06.2022).

Ruess, Julia, Gess, Christopher and Deicke, Wolfgang (2016) Forschendes Lernen und forschungsbezogene Lehre – empirisch gestützte Systematisierung des Forschungsbezugs der hochschulischen Lehre. In: *Zeitschrift für Hochschulentwicklung*, Vol. 11, No. 2, pp. 23-44. https://doi.org/10.3217/zfhe-11-02/02

Schneider, Beat (2005) *Design: eine Einführung*. Basel: Birkhäuser.

Schön, Donald A. (1983) *The Reflective Practitioner*. New York: Basic Books.

Schön, Donald A. (1987) *Educating the Reflective Practitioner*. San Francisco, CA: Jossey-Bass.

Schaper, Niclas (2012) *Fachgutachten zur Kompetenzorientierung in Studium und Lehre. HRK-Fachgutachten ausgearbeitet für die HRK von Niclas Schaper unter Mitwirkung von Oliver Reis und Johannes Wildt so wie Eva Horvath und Elena Bender*, August 2012 [online]. Available at: https://www.hrk-nexus.de/fileadmin/redaktion/hrk-nexus/07-Downloads/07-02-Publikationen/fachgutachten_kompetenzorientierung.pdf (accessed 29.06.2022).

Scrivener, Stephen A. R. (2002) The Art Object Does Not Embody a Form of Knowledge. In: *Working Papers in Art & Design*, Vol. 2 [online]. Available at: http://www.herts.ac.uk/_data/assets/pdf_file/0008/12311/WPIAAD_vol2_scrivener.pdf (accessed 29.06.2022).

Shreeve, Alison, Bailey, Sue and Drew, Linda (2003) Students' approaches to the 'research' component in the fashion design project: Variation in students' experience of the research process. In: *Art, Design & Communication in Higher Education*, Vol. 2, No. 3, pp. 113-130. https://doi.org/10.1386/adch.2.3.113/0

Simon, Herbert A. (1996) *The sciences of the artificial*. 3rd Edition, Cambridge, Mass.: MIT Press.

Steffen, Dagmar (2000) *Design als Produktsprache. Der „Offenbacher Ansatz" in Theorie und Praxis.* Frankfurt am Main: Verlag form GmbH.

Tonkinwise, Cameron and Vaughan, Laurene (2013) *Critiquing the North American Design PhD. A symposium exploring the institutional frameworks for practice- transforming design research.* Carnegie Mellon University, School of Design, 5. October 2013 [online]. Available at: https://phddesigncrit.files. wordpress.com/2013/04/critiquing-the-north-american-design-phd.pdf (accessed 29.06.2022).

Vaughan, Laurene (2019a) Embracing the Literacies of Design as Means and Mode of Dissemination. In: Vaughan, Laurene [ed.]: *Practice-based Design Research.* London, New York, Oxford, New Delhi, Sydney: Bloomsbury, pp. 111-118.

Vaughan, Laurene (2019b) Introducing Practiced-based Design Research. In: Vaughan, Laurene [ed.]: *Practice-based Design Research.* London, New York, Oxford, New Delhi, Sydney: Bloomsbury, pp. 1-6.

Vaughan, Laurene and Morrison, Andrew (2013) Form, fit and flair: considering the design doctorate. In: Reitan, Janne B., Lloyd, Peter, Bohemia, Erik, Nielsen, Elsebeth G., Digranes, Ingvild and Lutnæs, Eva [eds.]: DRS Cumulus Oslo 2013: *Design Learning for Tomorrow: Proceedings of the 2nd International Conference for Design Education Researchers.* Oslo, Norway, 14-17 May 2013, pp. 1819-1831 [online]. Available at: https://researchbank.rmit.edu.au/view/ rmit:23739 (accessed 29.06.2022).

Vaughan, Laurene and Morrison, Andrew (2014) Unpacking models, approaches and materialisations of the design PhD. In: *Studies in Material Thinking*, Vol. 11, pp. 3-19 [online]. Available at: https://www. academia.edu/8176079/Unpacking_models_ approaches_and_materialisations_of_the_design_PhD (accessed 29.06.2022).Verma, J. P. and Abdel-Salam, Abdel-Salam Gomaa (2019) *Testing Statistical Assumptions in Research.* Hoboken: John Wiley & Sons Inc. https://doi.org/10.1002/9781119528388

Wareham, Terry and Trowler, Paul (2007) *Deconstructing and Reconstructing 'The Teaching-Research Nexus': Lessons from Art and Design.* Presented at All Ireland Society for Higher Education Conference, National University Ireland, Maynooth [online]. Available at: https://paul-trowler.weebly.com/ uploads/4/2/4/3/42439197/deconstructing_and_ reconstructing_the_teaching-research_nexus-_ lessons_from_art_and_design.pdf (accessed 29.06.2022).

Weaver, Kathleen F., Morales, Vanessa, Dunn, Sarah L., Godde, Kanya and Weaver, Pablo F. (2017) *An Introduction to Statistical Analysis in Research: With Applications in the Biological and Life Sciences.* Hoboken: John Wiley & Sons Inc. https://doi. org/10.1002/9781119454205

Witzel, Andreas (2000) Das problemzentrierte Interview. In: *Forum Qualitative Sozialforschung*, Vol. 1, No. 1, Art. 22 [online]. Available at: https://www. qualitative-research.net/index.php/fqs/article/ view/1132/2520 (accessed 29.06.2022).

I1   Figures and Tables

Authors:

Univ.-Prof. Mag. Dr. <u>Sandra Dittenberger</u>, is full professor for Human-Centred Design and Design Research at New Design University in St. Pölten, Austria. As an industrial designer and design researcher, her research focuses on human-centred design process methodologies, socio-technical product development, design for human diversity, design for wellbeing and design education research.

Univ.-Prof. Mag. <u>Hans Stefan Moritsch</u>, is a designer and full professor at the New Design University in St. Pölten, where he has headed the Manual & Material Culture course since 2013. His research focuses on the connection between theory and practice in design education and the development of transitions between dual and tertiary education models.

<u>Agnes Raschauer</u>, Bakk. MA, is a sociologist, working at the University of Vienna and as research associate in the project "Research in Design Education". Her areas of work focus on qualitative methodology, university research, knowledge cultures and social inequality.

The study was realized with the support of the following institutions.

WISSENSCHAFT · FORSCHUNG
NIEDERÖSTERREICH

WKO NÖ
WIRTSCHAFTSKAMMER NIEDERÖSTERREICH

Die New Design University
ist die Privatuniversität
der Wirtschaftskammer NÖ
und ihres WIFI

NEW DESIGN
UNIVERSITY
PRIVATUNIVERSITÄT ST. PÖLTEN

Architektur und Design

Daniel Hornuff
Die Neue Rechte und ihr Design
Vom ästhetischen Angriff auf die offene Gesellschaft

2019, 142 S., kart., 17 SW-Abbildungen
19,99 € (DE), 978-3-8376-4978-9
E-Book:
PDF: 17,99 € (DE), ISBN 978-3-8394-4978-3

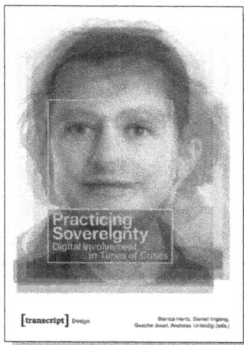

Bianca Herlo, Daniel Irrgang,
Gesche Joost, Andreas Unteidig (eds.)
Practicing Sovereignty
Digital Involvement in Times of Crises

January 2022, 430 p., pb., col. ill.
35,00 € (DE), 978-3-8376-5760-9
E-Book: available as free open access publication
PDF: ISBN 978-3-8394-5760-3

Christoph Rodatz, Pierre Smolarski (Hg.)
Wie können wir den Schaden maximieren?
Gestaltung trotz Komplexität.
Beiträge zu einem Public Interest Design

2021, 234 S., kart.
29,00 € (DE), 978-3-8376-5784-5
E-Book: kostenlos erhältlich als Open-Access-Publikation
PDF: ISBN 978-3-8394-5784-9

**Leseproben, weitere Informationen und Bestellmöglichkeiten
finden Sie unter www.transcript-verlag.de**

Architektur und Design

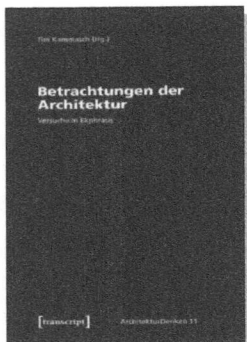

Tim Kammasch (Hg.)
Betrachtungen der Architektur
Versuche in Ekphrasis

2020, 326 S., kart., 63 SW-Abbildungen
30,00 € (DE), 978-3-8376-4994-9
E-Book:
PDF: 29,99 € (DE), ISBN 978-3-8394-4994-3

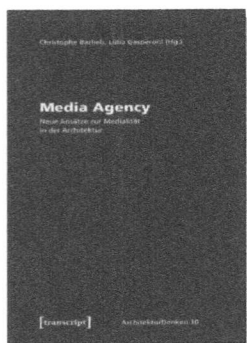

Christophe Barlieb, Lidia Gasperoni (Hg.)
**Media Agency –
Neue Ansätze zur Medialität in der Architektur**
2020, 224 S., Klappbroschur, 67 SW-Abbildungen
29,99 € (DE), 978-3-8376-4874-4
E-Book: kostenlos erhältlich als Open-Access-Publikation
PDF: ISBN 978-3-8394-4874-8

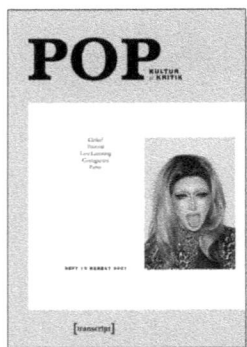

Thomas Hecken, Moritz Baßler, Elena Beregow,
Robin Curtis, Heinz Drügh, Mascha Jacobs,
Annekathrin Kohout, Nicolas Pethes, Miriam Zeh (Hg.)
POP
Kultur und Kritik (Jg. 10, 2/2021)

2021, 176 S., kart.
16,80 € (DE), 978-3-8376-5394-6
E-Book:
PDF: 16,80 € (DE), ISBN 978-3-8394-5394-0

GPSR Authorized Representative: Easy Access System Europe, Mustamäe tee 50, 10621 Tallinn, Estonia, gpsr.requests@easproject.com

www.ingramcontent.com/pod-product-compliance
Lightning Source LLC
Chambersburg PA
CBHW052112020426
42335CB00021B/2734